ONE POWERFUL MIND

THE COMPLETE APPROACH TO EMOTIONAL MANAGEMENT AT HOME AND AT WORK

PAUL WITZ

PRENTICE HALL CANADA
SCARBOROUGH, ONTARIO

Canadian Cataloguing in Publication Data

Witz, Paul
    One powerful mind: the complete approach to emotional
management at home and at work.

Includes index.

ISBN 0-13-929325-6

1. Emotional maturity.   2. Self-actualization (psychology).
I. Title.

BF710.W57 1998   158.1   C98-931902-4

 © 1998 Paul Witz

Prentice Hall Canada Inc.
Scarborough, Ontario
A Division of Simon & Schuster/A Viacom Company

Prentice-Hall, Inc., Upper Saddle River, New Jersey
Prentice-Hall International (UK) Limited, London
Prentice-Hall of Australia, Pty. Limited, Sydney
Prentice-Hall Hispanoamericana, S.A., Mexico City
Prentice-Hall of India Private Limited, New Delhi
Prentice-Hall of Japan, Inc., Tokyo
Simon & Schuster Southeast Asia Private Limited, Singapore
Editora Prentice-Hall do Brasil, Ltda., Rio de Janeiro

ISBN 0-13-929325-6

Director, Trade Group: Robert Harris
Copy Editor: Liba Berry
Assistant Editor: Joan Whitman
Production Coordinator: Shannon Potts
Art Direction: Mary Opper
Cover Design: Q30 Design Inc.
Interior Design: Julia Hall
Page Layout: Archetype

1 2 3 4 5 RRD 02 01 00 99 98

Printed and bound in Canada

Visit the Prentice Hall Canada Web site!
Send us your comments, browse our catalogues, and more.
www.phcanada.com

CONTENTS

This book is dedicated to all the children past, present, and future who were told that they can't.

ACKNOWLEDGMENTS

I would like to give special thanks to the following people:

To my wife, who believed in me and who encouraged me to get this book completed. One method of persuasion she used was to publish her own book first—and it worked. Also, I thank her for her patience during the hours I spent writing while insisting that she keep me company.

To my beautiful children, Greg, Peter, and Margot, who were so supportive during the writing of this book. I love you all deeply.

To my mother, who let me tell my story and supported me unconditionally.

To Paul MacMartin, my editor, for challenging me and for putting up with my ever-increasing demands. Your insights helped sculpt what has gone from a dream to reality.

To Liba Berry, my copy editor, thank you for your invaluable knowledge, humour, and sensitivity.

Thank you to Hart Hillman and Robert Harris of Prentice Hall Canada, who recognized the importance of my work—your support and commitment are very much appreciated.

And finally, thanks to the thousands of people who use the Emotional Management System every day and who show me that what I thought was right, was right. Without all of you, my dream could never have come true.

PREFACE

A powerful mind is not simply a mind that can solve complex problems. A powerful mind can solve problems in the midst of highly charged emotional situations. Each of us has the capacity to reach high levels of emotion; similarly, each of us has the capacity to reach higher levels of reason. This is not difficult under normal circumstances. What *is* difficult is managing the situations that generate strong emotion while they demand an equally elevated level of reason to manage effectively. The ability to integrate a high level of emotion with a high level of reason is what distinguishes the truly powerful, unified mind.

One of the most important advances in the area of human development is the newly defined category of emotional intelligence, or EQ. The essence of emotional intelligence is that the more effectively you integrate your emotional capacities with your rational capacities, the greater your active level of EQ. It was thrilling to discover the extensive research into emotional intelligence, but the studies and discussions on this intriguing area of human development did not say *how* a person could achieve this state of unified emotional-rational functioning.

This book focuses on a system that will help you achieve a unified mind. It explains how the Emotional Management System works and what makes it work. This system allows you to harness the natural processes of listening, investigating, pondering and taking action. It will enable you to let your rational capacity work with your emotional capacity so that you can consistently make constructive decisions. This book shows you how to use that perfect natural system to your advantage during times when your emotions shake that system out of alignment.

Psychological and psychiatric therapy largely focus on self-analysis. If you can trace back the system of thought and emotion that created your present state, you can certainly develop a system to balance it. I am not questioning the validity of the psychological approach, I am questioning its effectiveness and appropriateness in today's world. What we need is not to focus on the unnatural mental processes that make people behave chaotically and unreasonably, but to identify the emotional and rational human processes that are wholly natural and that function together harmoniously to allow people to achieve their goals.

Many individuals who seek psychological help do so prematurely. They suffer from the flawed assumption that they cannot use their natural inner power to solve their problems. *One Powerful Mind* urges you to rely on the natural process of personal transformation that exists within you. This book will help you find it, then apply it.

I have trained thousands of people to reach a Position of Independence by using the Emotional Management System. The purpose of the system is to use your powerful mind to re-establish the balance between the emotional and the rational. This system ensures that you function with a high level of emotional intelligence, and leaves you completely self-reliant. Unlike many medical and psychiatric approaches that encourage dependence on external supports like medication, the Emotional Management System liberates you from external supports. This is why I refer to the result of successfully applying the system as your Position of Independence. You achieve a fully independent and natural state of mind that allows you to act in your own best interests.

This book is divided into four parts:

Part 1 introduces you to the effects of the cavebrain, illustrates how we increasingly suffer from its domination over the computerbrain, and tests how close you are to an ideal pattern of emotional intelligence. Part 2 discusses the dynamics of the cavebrain and explains how you can map out a strategy for building a bridge between the cavebrain and computerbrain. Part 3 describes the seven steps of the Emotional Management System, and provides you with strategies to increase your emotional intelligence. Part 4 provides examples of how people apply the Emotional Management System in actual situations.

There is a Native American saying that many of us stoically accept. It says "What cannot be altered must be endured." I offer you a new saying: "That power you use to endure is the same power you can use to transform your life." The Emotional Management System will help you achieve an inner peace and feeling of accomplishment you have hoped for but never dreamed possible.

PART I

CAVEBRAIN REACTIONS IN A POSTMODERN WORLD

INTRODUCTION

SNAKES IN THE GRASS

I was in trouble. Deep, deep trouble. My business was at a crossroads. My career was at a crossroads. And most excruciating of all, my marriage was at a crossroads. I had done something I never in my wildest dreams imagined I could or would do: I had separated from my wife and children.

I was a mess. My life was moving headlong towards change, but I had no idea what that change would be. I was confused, anxious, and indecisive. I had to make a decision about my marriage, but that crucial decision eluded me. I know that if it were not for the emotional intelligence skills I had developed over the previous twenty-five years, I would have fallen apart.

ATTACK OF THE CAVEBRAIN

When I need to get away from it all, I play golf. I walk along the fragrant, quiet fairways enjoying the serenity of the rolling green hills; that is, of course, until I hook one or slice one off into the woods or the deep rough. And I do that frequently, especially when I'm upset. Which makes me more upset. Getting away from it all and ending up frustrated may strike you as counter-productive, but consider this: the activity allows me to stop thinking so much and start feeling something, even if that feeling is frustration. Deep feeling is deeply important.

It's amazing. You never know just what experience in life will awaken a realization within you, do you? But when it happens you know it, and often it puts your entire life and your life's work in perspective in an instant. I had one of these seminal experiences on the eleventh hole, hunting for my ball in the rough after a typical slice off the tee.

Hoping against hope to find my ball, I ventured into the first cut of rough then into the hip-deep stuff and started to peck around with my wedge. I turned around to forage in a tuft of grass and reached in with my club. That's when something slid up on me from behind. A snake! I could feel its sinister vibration as it prepared to put me out of my misery.

I leapt at least forty feet in the air. I howled. I flailed my arms at my attacker. Somehow I had to keep my slithery executioner from delivering the coup de grâce. I didn't want to die. Not here, not on a golf course, for crying out aloud!

By that time my golf partner, Steve, had hoofed it across the fairway and stationed himself a few feet away from me. He peered at me intently, clearly confused. He didn't come any closer. Some friend! There I stood, confronted by a lethal snake, and he squints at me stupidly.

Then, just as suddenly as the attack occurred, it dawned on me that I had not been attacked by a snake; I had reacted with hair-raising fear to my new vibrating pager. I plucked it from my belt and held it aloft. Steve began to laugh hysterically, leaning on his knees with both hands to keep himself from falling down.

My heart was pounding. My ankle hurt from jumping around hacking away at the phantom reptile. I was tired. And out of breath. And I felt stupid and embarrassed. Then the absurdity of the situation struck me and I started to laugh along with Steve. We laughed for a couple of minutes until the guys on the tee started hollering at us to get moving. I took a penalty stroke and hacked back onto the fairway and completed my round.

DOES EMOTION MAKE US STUPID?

On the way back home I thought about my phantom snake in the grass. I was relieved that no one had been there to witness my initial reaction. If Steve had been ball hunting with me at the moment of the "attack," I am sure I would have brained him with my pitching wedge. There I was, the founder of a successful training institute, convinced I was being attacked by a snake, when I was being attacked by my pager. How dense, I thought. How stupid.

Why had I reacted so dramatically? I asked myself. I decided that I was responding to an innate sense of self-preservation. I also decided that had I spent two seconds examining the situation, I would have realized the truth and thus avoided the phantom-reptile death struggle, a story that will no doubt follow me for the rest of my golfing days. But I didn't take the two seconds to review the situation and make a more intelligent response. I didn't have those two seconds. I was saving my life and there was no time to think.

I make light of the episode now only because ultimately I was able to clearly identify my misperception. It came to a slapstick conclusion, but make no mistake, I was terrified when I was sure I was in danger. My reality told me that I was in mortal danger and I reacted accordingly. This episode highlights the fascinating way that emotion works when it is fully engaged: it immediately eliminates all rational input and allows you to perform at a near-automatic level in order to meet your most primal needs immediately. The emotional mind is turned on and the rational mind is turned off.

Most of all, my encounter with the "snake" highlighted for me the simple facts behind what I had perceived to be the complex issues surrounding my marriage. The insights I gleaned from my experience on that golf course got me thinking, and helped me see a way to make my marriage work. My wife, Marion, and I have since worked through the issues that were keeping us apart, and we are together again. Working through these issues and using the Emotional Management System inspired me to document the dynamics of the system in this book, and to record the extensive observations about emotion and reason that have been the foundation of my work for more than twenty-five years.

GAMBLING WITH YOUR EMOTIONS

The phantom-snake episode clearly illustrates how emotion functions in an emergency. But what happens when your life isn't actually in immediate mortal danger, or even in *perceived* immediate mortal danger? What happens when you become highly emotional, even though you have time to evaluate a situation? Do you stop, and automatically introduce rational thought into the equation? Or docs that cavebrain type of emotion take over and make you do things that end up embarrassing you, or worse, cause serious consequences?

Unfortunately, that cavebrain attack happens to us far more often than any of us would care to admit. Observe for a moment a casual gambler playing the card game Twenty-One. The stakes are low: 50 cents a hand. The player—we'll call him John—has developed a wagering system that works for him about seven times out of ten. After seven hours he has accumulated $250, a phenomenal improvement over his initial wagers. It took time, patience, and a system or method of playing to achieve these results.

The next day John returns to the casino excited about the success of his system. He has figured out that instead of betting 50 cents a hand, he should increase the stakes to $150 per stake. John has calculated that, based on his previous performance, a 250 percent improvement on the initial investment will be very suitable indeed. It sounds like a wildly dramatic increase in wagering, doesn't it?

John sits down at the table and begins playing his hands with wagers of $150. The hands start well enough: the first is a winner, so is the second. The third is a losing hand, only this time the loss isn't 50 cents; it's $150. The next hand is another loss, followed by a win. Then another loss. Within one hour, John has lost more than $750. He has lost everything

What happened? John's strong primal fear told him that he could suddenly not afford to lose more than he could win, so he became extremely stressed. Not only did this stress distort John's objective, but because of the dominance of his emotions John veered away from his method of wagering and card selection so often that he ended up following no system at all. He attempted to compensate with a new approach. His new approach, however, wasn't dictated by logic, but by emotion. With each win and loss, more and more emotions came into play, which, together with a variance of method, led John to make a reckless and desperate attempt to win back all his money quickly. He lost the lot.

If John had continued to follow his original and extremely successful wagering and card selection system when the stakes were only 50 cents, the outcome would likely have been different when he was playing with the larger wagers. There would certainly have been more stability and control. The status of the stake became more precarious with the introduction of emotions.

Erratic decision making based on emotions alone creates circumstances which are invariably contrary to those you intend, which also invariably creates unnecessary difficulties. This is the nature of emotion. It doesn't matter how intelligent you are or how high your IQ is. When feelings such as anger, despondency, fear, excitement, or infatuation, or a combination of emotions, overtake a situation, you begin to think things, say things, and do things that are diametrically opposed to your own best interests. You lose sight of your objective, or you generate pain or tragedy in your life. You lose power because your emotional mind is not allowing your rational mind to help you out.

THE PAIN OF TWO SOLITUDES

Romantic relationships are prime arenas for observing the destructive power of unmanaged emotion. Strife erupts so easily and quickly when each person in the relationship becomes so embroiled in their own emotions that they become blinded to each other's individual needs and the mutual needs that will sustain them as a couple.

Consider a couple with whom my wife and I recently had dinner. Marion and I were looking forward to spending a quiet evening with Jake and Leanne. They had been married and divorced before meeting each other, and both had children by previous marriages. Jake's kids live with their mother, but Leanne's children lived with Leanne and Jake. Leanne carries a tremendous amount of stress and guilt concerning every aspect of her children's lives. She compensates for her feelings by being, as she describes it, overprotective of them and giving them everything they want.

The evening started off pleasantly, and things were going quite well until we sat down for coffee and cake in the living room after dinner. Conversation quickly evolved into an unfortunate session of he said/she said concerning the missing cherries on the cake; Jake had accused the children of stealing the cherries. This rapidly escalated into a venomous knock-down drag-out argument that obviously had no relevance to the comparative importance of the lack of cherries on top of the dessert. It may sound incongruous, but I know that these two have a tremendous amount of affection for each other. And when the couple is away from Leanne's kids, they are openly affectionate with each other. However, there they were, ripping strips off each other, and there seemed to be only a sinew of connection remaining between them. It always amazes me how quickly emotions can corrupt a moment and how, once people are embroiled in argument, they begin to spew forth nasty and cruel distortions of facts.

Needless to say, Marion and I felt extremely awkward, and we both felt badly for these two intelligent, upset people. They were like railway cars running in different directions on different tracks and never connecting, and it was destroying them both. Leanne, who by now was a complete prisoner to her intense rage, began lashing out and nearly screaming, "Did you hear what he just said! Do you see how he gets over a lousy cake! Do you know that it's just the same way he treats my children! Do you know that no one likes him! My sister hates him. My children can't stand to be near him. Can you believe this man!"

Her accusations tumbled out, each running into the next. Her thinking was completely dominated by her primal emotions of anger and resentment. Her reaction toward her husband was based on her commitment to protect her children, which was mainly based on guilt.

At this point these two people were destroying each other and they didn't have a hope of reconnecting. There was no balance between their strong and powerful emotions and their obviously equally strong and powerful intelligence. There was plenty of emotion and plenty of button-pushing and verbal attacks, but there was no integration of the two. Their emotion and reason were not working together, even though these capacities were functioning simultaneously. Jake and Leanne were functioning as two solitudes, and as a result their relationship was functioning the same way.

Such relationships suffer from a near-complete absence of emotional management, and it becomes nearly impossible for either person in the relationship to view their situation, as individuals and as a couple, with objectivity. Arguments flare then rage to the point of destruction with a speed that seems impossible to control. Emotions take over and, before you know what's happening, the damage is done, and all you are left with are fragile justifications for the emotional carnage that a lack of emotional management has produced.

Jake and Leanne stopped arguing for a moment and looked at me. It became clear that however distorted the situation was between them, and regardless of who was right and who was wrong, these two combatants needed to find a common ground so as to avert further emotional carnage. With their gazes trained on me, they were inviting me into the brouhaha at which I had, until that point, been merely an uncomfortable spectator.

"Well?" Leanne said to me.

"Well," I responded, "help him. Reach out and help him understand. Simply smacking him on the head, what good does that do? How does that help? It doesn't. So try to help him understand. Reach out. Now, if he is wrong—and for argument's sake let's say he is—the fact that you are simply telling him he's wrong does nothing to improve your own situation or his. Reach out and say, 'Let me help you understand how to do something differently.' But you've got to have the insight and the inner force and inner strength to be able to do this reaching out."

The reason behind my observations and simple suggestions appeared to be lost on her. She sat there stone-faced. Here was the classic paradox: Leanne was trying to find a way to resolve the situation between her and Jake, which meant that she still considered them a couple. Nevertheless, her reaction of attacking him displayed that she didn't want him near her. She was not finding it possible to integrate her important rational reasoning capacities with her equally important and meaningful emotional reactions. As a result, she was going nowhere and was burning herself up inside in the process.

Jake was struggling with his own distorted understanding of the dynamic between him and Leanne, and was similarly unable to integrate his reasoning capacity with his intense emotions. By this point, he was so upset that he had withdrawn completely and appeared to be close to tears. Jake faulteringly said to me, "You know, Paul, whatever I say is wrong, because whatever I do is wrong. I can do no right."

It was a long, teary-eyed night that left Marion and I exhausted and looking forward to returning to our home and to our rambunctious children and their rooms that they never want to clean up, and pestering dogs and cats, and the clothes dryer on the fritz. Leanne and Jake are perfect examples of people who need the Emotional Management System. Happily, they have begun to apply the approach to the issues they confront as a couple.

What would typically happen in a situation like the one described above? Eventually, the couple would split up. Or, if they had a little more on the ball, they might introduce a third party such as a friend or a counsellor to try to facilitate the integration of emotion and reason by showing the pair how to bridge the two strong capacities so that they could save their relationship. But think about this kind of solution for a moment. Bringing someone else into the situation to facilitate reconciliation removes the responsibility from the two individuals and deposits it on the third party. This approach, even if it brings the couple closer together, produces an unpleasant result: it plants the suggestion in the minds of the troubled individuals that they do not have the skills to resolve their own problems.

For the most part I do not support the third-party approach. After all, what happens when a third party contributes to the problem rather than to the solution, which was the case with Leanne and Jake when their counsellor sided with one party over the other. Besides, can you always rely on a third party to be there for you whenever you need them? Can this individual always know the deepest parts of you that only you know and can identify? And isn't it more powerful to be in control of your own life than to hand that control to someone else? Shouldn't self-respect be the permanent by-product of achieving resolutions to your own problems? Wouldn't it be better if you were self-reliant? Wouldn't it be better if you could correct things before you go so off the track that you need an outside resource to help you try to find your way back? Wouldn't this be the evidence of a mind so powerful that it can function with exceptional reason even when it is functioning with exceptional emotion.

It is better to be self-reliant, and if you are facing a situation that you don't think you know how to handle, read this book carefully. It will teach you a system for integrating your intellect and your emotion that will give you an indispensable tool to manage yourself and your life: a powerful, unified mind.

MANAGING CAVEBRAIN ATTACKS

When you're in the throes of an argument with a loved one, and you feel that you're headed for disaster, do you have the situation in perspective? Probably not. What about when you're due for your annual performance review, and even though you do great work, you've convinced yourself that your inadequacies will jeopardize your advancement? Is there anything you can do? Do you feel utterly helpless?

At times, most of us do feel as if we have lost control over our lives. We suffer terrible internal pain, believing our perceived failures to be unique. We believe we have no power over the snakes in the grass that seem to be ruining our lives. Nothing could be further from the truth.

The fact is, we just don't know how to get back on track. We get caught in a state of sustained reaction. We haven't had a proven set of procedures to rely on to get ourselves back in control and start creating our own destinies instead of allowing destiny to control us. We have never learned to deal correctly with the emotional winds that derail us and leave us painfully far from our destination. After all, such skills are not taught in school, most parents have no structured way to impart these skills, and life experiences tend to entrench less-than-effective life skills rather than serve as lessons for growth. I believe that we all know intuitively that there must be a way to regain control: there has to be a way, because we sense the need for change.

UNDERSTANDING PERSONAL EVOLUTION

This sense you get that there must be a better way is all the proof you need of your intrinsic, intuitive wisdom. Because you're right. You can control your life. You can create your own destiny. You can be the person you want to be and achieve the goals you've set. You may not be able to be rational and logical when faced with an emotional encounter. This is to be expected. You are not a robot. But what you *can* do is decide what you are going to do with your emotions. You can learn to manage them. You can learn to monitor them and steer them and transform them from a self-destructive force into the fire that drives your life. You can learn to increase your rational functioning when your emotions are trying to rule your world.

Perhaps your perceived shortcomings are simply the result of a lack of skills training in managing this inner fire. Have you ever asked yourself why you do the things you do when so often they end up messing things up? Is it stupidity? Is it masochism? Or could it be something deeper, something primordial? Perhaps it is something so deeply embedded in your emotional coding that you find it impossible to put your finger on it, let alone manage on your own. We are a species controlled by our most basic instincts. We apply "prehistoric" human capacities in contexts in which they don't belong. For all the pride we take in our achievements as a civilization, we have largely underestimated the power of our primal emotional reactions and how they influence our behaviour. We haven't learned how to manage the one human component that gives us the fire to live life fully and intensely.

Civilization is a relatively recent phenomenon. Our essential wiring was created in our cave-dwelling days. And what is the legacy left by our cave ancestors? The cavebrain—the propensity to react like a caveman or a cavewoman, right in the middle of our modern lives. The Emotional Management System enables you to integrate fundamental emotional motivations with an advanced ability to develop strategies to attain life goals. The goal of the Emotional Management System is not to eliminate strong emotions. Emotions are the core of what it is to be human. Emotions show you what has true meaning in life. Emotions are essential. When people say they have trouble with their emotions, they are usually unintentionally misspeaking. Emotions are actually performing perfectly as intended: intensely and clearly. The area of concern is not emotions, but how to integrate rational thought with strong emotions to make meaningful decisions that meet your best interests and the best interests of those around you.

The Emotional Management System is based on a remarkably elementary skill: being smart about your emotions in order to increase emotional intelligence. And what is emotional intelligence? Emotional intelligence is thinking and then acting intelligently about your emotions. It is the integration of emotional and rational thought forged to create a greater force. And if you are going to be smart about your emotions, you need to recognize and understand how emotion operates and affects your thinking and behaviour. It is the key to unleashing the complete power of your mind. It is the first step to making the kinds of changes that will change your life.

Journal Entry

Can it be that I begin
To lose control
Feel sick
In the pit of my stomach
How can a nontangible feeling
Cause me
So much real pain
Although at the moment I know
Not what I am in the darkness of despair
I will search for my light of day
And even if I never find it
May I die trying
For that is far better than
Accepting who I am.

1

THE SURVIVAL MOTIVE

Self-preservation is the primary instinct of all sentient beings. We are creatures programmed to save our own skin. Sometimes this survival motive helps us; at other times it is our worst enemy. And although we face so few natural dangers compared to our cave-dwelling ancestors, our reaction patterns are often remarkably primitive and out of step with the problems we regularly face. Why do we behave this way? It is simply because we still tend to react to interpersonal challenges as if they were natural mortal dangers. Indeed, our brain is designed to perform this way. Its prime function is to ensure our survival first, and later reflect and consider events.

TWO BRAINS IN ONE

In order to achieve one powerful mind, you need to understand that you actually have two brains: one that feels and one that thinks. There is a distinct difference between which brain works first when faced with an "emotional" situation. Because of the architecture of our brains, it is our feeling mind that operates first in all situations, followed shortly by our thinking, rational brain.

The Amygdala (Your Cavebrain)

Here is how it all works. The brain's most basic component is the *brain stem*, which surrounds the top of the spinal cord. We share this fundamental brain structure with the vast majority of earth species. This root brain regulates basic life functions like respiration and the operation of our other organs. It also controls our reactions and movements—the internally coded monitors that make sure the body operates properly and that make possible the emotional reactions that ensure our survival.

Perched to the left and right of the brain stem is the *amygdala*, two small almond-shaped structures that act as a kind of hard drive that stores emotional memory. It may be a small part of the brain, but it is the part that stores emotional meaning. Because of its primal importance, the amygdala has the ability to take control of brain functions, even preempt the functions of higher thought.

I have named this part of the brain the *cavebrain*—the engine that drives primal reactions. Its functions are immediate and completely reactive. We need it to make the split-second reactions that ensure self-preservation and survival. These reactions are very important. They have been the core component of our survival system for millions of years. Although we don't face the kinds of dangers our ancestors had to confront, we still face a number of physical dangers every day. For the most part, we manage them pretty well. For example, when you're driving and another driver flies out at you from the other side of the road, there is no time to consider an alternative; in a millisecond you swerve and avoid the oncoming car and avoid other vehicles and obstructions as well. This is the amygdala at work.

In addition to physical dangers, we also face emotional dangers. These internal disturbances can be traumatic because when we fail to manage them effectively we have to live with the consequences. Nevertheless, the cavebrain still functions the same way. It is all about feeling, and reacting automatically in order to secure self-preservation. The cavebrain is what kicked in when I believed I was being attacked by the snake and started whacking my club around at absolutely nothing before I even knew what I was doing.

Chapter 1

THE CAVEBRAIN'S REIGN OF TERROR

The all-feeling amygdala doesn't just make life-saving, split-second reactions. The cavebrain is also the storehouse for emotional meaning. Any sensory input that triggers emotion will be processed by the cavebrain in a deeply reactive manner. Consider Aileen, an anorectic girl who weighed only 82 pounds at the time of her death. Aileen was a bright young woman of 23 who came from a prosperous family. She had enrolled in university and was studying law. Aileen's intense fear of and hatred for obesity had become so instilled in the emotional meaning reservoir of her amygdala that she was unable to accurately process considerations about her weight—through her *neocortex*—that part of the brain I call the *computerbrain*. When she was in front of a mirror, the painfully thin Aileen would see a fat person and intensify her self-induced pattern of starvation.

Many of us would attribute such a distorted perception as a failure of the computerbrain to process the information correctly, but the cavebrain is the culprit. Aileen was so afraid of gaining weight that the cavebrain would not allow her neocortex and its advanced rational capacities to arrive at the conclusion that appeared obvious to everyone around her. In this way, the cavebrain is functioning efficiently, to a fault. It was directing Aileen to do whatever it took to ensure her self-preservation, paradoxically even if it killed her. Aileen was reacting without the capacity to think about the consequences of those reactions.

Reacting without thought gets you and me into a lot of trouble a lot of the time. The chasm between cavebrain emotion and rational thought can frequently cause serious difficulties in our lives and prevent us from realizing our goals. You will soon know how to prevent this kind of trouble as you learn to restrain the cavebrain's reactionary tendencies. That means integrating the functioning of our second brain—the neocortex—the one that generates and manages higher thought.

The Neocortex (Your Computerbrain)

The neocortex is the part of the brain that makes us distinctly human. It is what makes sense of all the information gathered by our five senses. This is the brain that *thinks* about feeling, and it is what enables us to analyze and process the information processed by the amygdala (the cavebrain) so that we can have feelings about the feelings we experience.

The computerbrain is linked to the primitive yet essential cavebrain, but it can operate virtually independent of the cavebrain. And it operates on a kind of delayed-reaction basis. It kicks in after the emotional brain has had its turn first. For example, the computerbrain is the component that finally determined that I wasn't being attacked by a snake last spring when I was playing golf, but by my own vibrating pager. And it's the component that made me and my golf partner laugh and continues to make lots of people laugh when the embarrassing story is told.

We developed our emotional brain long before we developed our rational one. The amygdala (cavebrain) is the first part of the brain to act, followed by the neocortex (computerbrain) and its analytical and reflective capacities (if the cavebrain allows information to run through it). Ideally in our day-to-day interactions the two brain capacities work in harmony, the cavebrain generating input, the computerbrain analyzing that input and developing appropriate conclusions and responses. Unfortunately, it doesn't operate in the natural way when emotions so barrage us that the computerbrain gets shut out, and we end up thinking, saying, and doing things that, in a "rational" state we would never consider emotionally intelligent.

SURVIVAL RESPONSES

We frequently overreact to situations. The cavebrain generates a reaction to a "new" reality, a situation that has never been evaluated effectively by the computerbrain. How often have you reacted to something without knowing all the facts, then regretted your reaction? It happens frequently and is, arguably, the number-one reason that so many people destroy their relationships and abandon their goals. These people react to unexpected input as if it were a mortal attack.

How do you know if you are facing such a situation? You'll recognize it when you feel fear, guilt, anger, hatred, even love, and act on it preemptively, before you've investigated the situation thoroughly. It emerges, for example, when we are asked to stand up and speak in front of a group of people at a seminar or meeting. It happens in the office or at home when we are criticized for making a mistake. It happens when you begin to consider questions like, "What if I lose my job?" or "What if I say the wrong thing?"

In such cases we often act first and never consider the appropriateness of our actions. We suffer a setback in life, it dominates our emotions, and we become ruled by this sustained level of futile emotion. It is as if evolution has not yet given humans the capacity to distinguish between events that threaten life and events that threaten well-being. This kind of self-deception may work well for us for a little while until our internal and interpersonal world starts to crumble. Our self-preservation motive has run amok.

DEFINING MORTAL DANGER

The trouble with the primitive self-preservation motive is that although it is necessary from time to time, most often it is not necessary at all. Certainly when you encounter a snake, you experience a "fight-or-flight" response. And you know enough from the bumps and bruises you earned as a kid that if you ride your bicycle recklessly and run into a pole or a curb or a parked car, you will hurt yourself. Experience and instinct taught you what to do and what not to do.

When we are faced with interpersonal challenges, however, our cavebrain often reacts as if they were mortal dangers. The emotional mind convinces the rational mind that the mortal dangers are real because the pain is real, and the computerbrain is unable to override this conclusion. Too often we do not know how to deal with these inputs. We do not know how to make the transition from cavebrain to computerbrain thinking. We mistake computerbrain challenges for cavebrain challenges and react more quickly than necessary. So, often these challenges persist, kept active by the demands of modern life: work, family, friends, finances. We create a sustained system of pressures without an equal system of internal capacities to handle them.

THE TYRANNY OF COMPUTERBRAIN DENIAL

We inherently understand that we often overreact to situations that require an integration of cavebrain and computerbrain processing. We do not try to balance our intense cavebrain reactions by giving them credence and then using our higher computerbrain functions to arrive at balanced responses. Instead, we deny the validity of our emotions altogether and rely only on our contemplative capacities. How does this phenomenon manifest itself? It most commonly appears when people who see us upset or in pain try to comfort us by saying things like, "Don't worry," "Just count to ten," "It will soon blow over," "Everything happens for the best," or "Oh, it's nothing." Your cavebrain experience is discounted. You are encouraged to disengage from your feelings because people don't think there is an alternative. Internal or interpersonal survival is a far less respected motive for emotional response because you and others cannot physically see the source of the threat confronting you.

You have probably experienced a trauma that has left you upset and disturbed, and someone says to you, "I know it hurts, but time will heal all. It will soon be over." In their protective capacity, people want to insulate you from the unpleasant feelings that arise in times of crisis. But pain and fear are natural. They serve a crucial role in emotional growth. Yes, it is a counterintuitive notion that pain and fear contributes to self-understanding. But you need pain. It provides you with the context for meaning in life. Primal emotions are essential to the process of working through the situations in your life that seem to keep you from moving forward, improving your condition, and being happy. Pain is the most obvious primal emotion that shapes your condition. It alerts you to the dangers around you, it activates the survival motive, and it sets the foundation for you to move forward and succeed.

THE ALTERNATIVE TO RESTRICTIVE SURVIVAL REACTIONS

My back has always given me problems. Recently I suffered a severe and prolonged back injury that restricted my movements for over a month. The tremendous pain I experienced required me to perform an entirely new set of exercises in addition to my normal daily regimen. I was warned that if I didn't do the exercises, I would likely have to undergo disk surgery.

The pain was my quintessential survival motive—a cavebrain emotion and perfectly natural. The muscles go into spasm in order to protect me, because otherwise I would likely go ahead and carry out my normal activities, which would do more damage to my back. The cavebrain reactions linked to survival motive were doing their job. Every time I attempted to use my back in any manner at that time, the pain was so severe that the only relief was to stop what I was doing.

If I had started reacting to the major symptom (pain), I simply would have made efforts to eliminate it and done nothing to regain my mobility. My goal was not only to be pain free, but also to become fully functional. And studies have proven that the back needs to be carefully realigned through specific exercises in order to recover from an injury. To do nothing but react to back pain and remain motionless leads to chronic symptomatic pain and possible permanent damage.

Let's consider the pain for a moment. We would much rather not experience any pain at all, given the choice. Pain, however, was the key emotion that led me to find the system that would ultimately help me. The pain restricted me and prevented me from attempting motions that would cause me to experience even more severe pain and possibly result in permanent damage. It was only through pain that I was protected. It helped me identify the problem and begin to use my computerbrain to make conscious decisions that would help me recover from my injury.

When you think about it, anything that is there to protect is also there to restrict. I am terrified to let my 13-year-old daughter out on her own in the city, so I become overprotective and I restrict her movements. In effect, I imprison her. Similarly, in my native country, South Africa, homes were fortified with iron bars on windows and doors in order to protect residents from attack during the riots and frequent break-in attempts during the height of unrest in that country. This is the unique nature of many of our cavebrain's survival motive reactions: they lock us in, imprisoning us in the very situation we need to escape.

When you are suffering the throes of cavebrain emotion, you face two primary options. Option one: you can decide to maintain the status quo, which will likely intensify your cavebrain emotion no matter what it is—fear or anger or pain. Option two: you can withdraw completely from the source of the problem in the hope that avoidance will protect you. When you take options one and two, you imprison yourself in a restricted life space that takes you nowhere.

Whether you recognize the fact or not, one of the reasons you are reading this book is that intuitively you recognize that options one and two are really non-options. There must be a third option, you decide, and you recognize that you must find it. You cannot remain in this restricted life space. You recognize that you need to relax enough to attend to the cause of your cavebrain emotion, and therefore you find yourself open to considering the third option: you can find a way to use your natural abilities to create a new approach. You focus on procedures that bring you into balance and work toward preventing the discomfort of cavebrain reactions. You consider a system that could manage not only your cavebrain reactions but also the patterns of thought and action that generate the conditions that result in cavebrain reactions. You move to a new level of balance in life, and this is how you begin to prepare yourself for the Emotional Management System.

Journal Entry

The animal instinct in man
comes to the fore
when his fellow man weakens.
Does the meditative animal
become man?
Does lion lie with lamb,
and man with nature?

THE SELF-BETTERMENT MOTIVE

Humans want to do more than survive; they want to thrive. We are not satisfied with the status quo. We continually strive for more. We want it all: health and wealth and happiness. We want our lives to get better, and we want the lives of those around us to improve too. We are never satisfied. That is part of what it is to be human. This inherent and instinctive drive is the self-betterment motive. It is the glimmer of light that keeps us pushing forward in our darkest hours, that draws us ever onwards to greater achievements and successes.

THE HIGHER COMPUTERBRAIN

It is through dissatisfaction that we grow, improve, overcome, and thrive. Dissatisfaction, however, is not an attribute of the cavebrain and its reactive nature. It reigns in the neocortex, the computerbrain. Why, then, does personal growth appear to arise from our sense of dissatisfaction and not from our sense of satisfaction? What accounts for our apparent programmed desire to better our condition?

PROBLEM SOLVING AND THE COMPUTERBRAIN

Our history as a species chronicles our dissatisfaction with our environment and our efforts to improve it and ourselves. When our computerbrain evaluates an area in our lives that needs improvement, it considers the problem and eventually proposes a solution or a series of solutions that could fulfill the need for self-betterment.

Paradoxically, even satisfaction is generally dissatisfying. You know how it goes: if something is going great, then it could be going greater. Why do world-class athletes like Wayne Gretzky, Michael Jordon, and Donovan Bailey strive to break their own records? Why do successful entrepreneurs like Bill Gates, Donald Trump, and Rupert Murdoch drive themselves to expand their already huge business empires? These people are already rich, so money can't be the motive. The drive toward self-improvement goes well beyond a desire for material gain. At the most basic level it is that once a goal is reached, it is time to strive again, not because there is an external force that requires the new effort, but because the drive to self-betterment is a fundamental human motive. Human beings are hard-wired to succeed.

The computerbrain is all about learning and solving problems. In our earliest cavebrain days we not only used our prime survival motive to maintain our lives, we also began to notice which solutions were consistently more effective than others. As explained in Chapter 1, the neocortex (computerbrain) is fed data to process only after the amygdala (cavebrain) has completed its instinctive reaction. But the computerbrain eventually gets hold of the data, processes it, arrives at conclusions and solutions, and determines new courses of action. Once we learn an effective solution, we incorporate it into our consciousness, and then focus on a new unresolved challenge and tackle it the same way.

YOUR PAIN IS OFTEN YOUR GAIN

Even though we continually strive for those perfect days when all goes smoothly and we haven't a care in the world, often we can barely recall what we learned from those periods of peace and happiness. It's as if once we reach one of these plateaus, life becomes curiously stagnant. On the other hand, we can nearly always remember the events that cause us pain and anguish. Think back. If you're like me, you don't have to think back all that far to recall a painful moment—a setback, a disappointment, a trauma. Ironically, we learn our great life lessons from these painful events.

Have you ever wondered why this is the case? Could it be that this is the way we grow? Could it be that your propensity to use your higher computerbrain to solve problems is what helps you to better yourself? If so, doesn't this tell you something profound about your life and your abilities? Doesn't it tell you that the struggles you face are actually the life material you need to mature to ever-greater levels?

When you are faced with powerfully troubling situations, the computerbrain can only execute its higher thinking and problem-solving functions after the cavebrain has completed its reactive process. You react before you can respond. It is not surprising, therefore, that people generally have such trouble responding intelligently and effectively to an interpersonal crisis.

IQ AND EMOTIONAL INTELLIGENCE

Look no further than Theodore J. Kaczynski, aka the Unabomber, whose delivery of 16 pipe bombs in the mail to unsuspecting targets led to 3 deaths and 23 serious injuries, and made him one of the world's most feared serial killers.

What makes Kaczynski such a terrifyingly fascinating study is that he was a remarkably intelligent man. Born to a successful and respected family in the suburbs of Chicago, Kaczynski was a prodigy. At the age of 12 he routinely defeated his parents' university-educated friends at Scrabble. He was an academic overachiever in his high school physics and math classes, and was a technically excellent, if rather unexpressive, trombone player in his high school band.

Kaczynski graduated from Harvard University in 1962, earned a master's degree in mathematics from the University of Michigan in 1964, and a Ph.D. in 1967. He didn't socialize with his fellow students, however, and those who knew him found it nearly impossible to carry on conversations with him. When he became an assistant professor at the University of California at Berkeley in 1967, students described his lectures as "useless." He dealt with students' questions by simply pretending that he hadn't heard any.

In 1971, Kaczynski left academia for a reclusive lifestyle in Montana where he built a shack on a small parcel of land in the forest outside the town of Lincoln. Seven years later, this man launched a reign of terror that is one of the most stunning examples of misplaced genius ever.

During his trial, Kaczynski steadfastly refused to enter a plea of guilty by reason of insanity. We may never discover what deep emotions were unable to integrate with this man's superior intelligence. In the end, his tremendous intellect enabled him to manifest these emotions in the deadliest manner possible.

When you consider Theodore Kaczynski, it is easy to see how a lack of emotional intelligence is no intelligence at all.

MINDING YOUR EMOTIONAL NEUTRAL ZONE

People commonly find themselves in the emotional neutral zone when things are in the process of going wrong. They haven't quite gone wrong yet, but they are on their way to doing so. The computerbrain is still very active, trying to find solutions. Surprisingly, however, you will not attempt to learn what you perceive you already know. The more you think you know, the less likely you are to look for alternative answers. It is this approach that proves to be the most damaging when it comes to your particular problem.

Consider taking driving lessons now, after you have been a driver for years. When you know how to drive, the idea seems preposterous. Why would you attempt to learn what you already know? You don't need to. You are in a zone of confidence and certainty. And if for some reason you were forced or obliged to take driving lessons, how patient would you likely be in such a situation? Will you hear half of what the instructor says? Or will you dismiss most it as irrelevant and a waste of time because you believe you already know how to drive?

Alter the dynamic for a moment and you may find yourself in the neutral zone. Example: your company sends you to work and live in a new country where people drive on the opposite side of the road and have unfamiliar traffic laws. And your new job requires that you drive extensively and immediately upon your arrival. You are now faced with the prospect of being tested in order to get a valid driver's licence. It seems like such an inane thing to have to do, but after running a stop sign because you were looking on the wrong side of the road, then colliding with another vehicle, the prospect of relearning to drive doesn't seem so preposterous anymore. Suddenly, you recognize your deficiencies.

Chapter 2

IDENTIFYING WHY THINGS WORK FOR YOU

Unfortunately, many of us not only recognize deficiencies where there are none, we just as often fail to recognize the many efficiencies of cavebrain-computerbrain integration.

Your cavebrain can often attack your self-image by its emotional conclusions, but in certain areas of your life, you may manage your cavebrain's tendencies far more effectively than you are aware of. It is in these areas that your cavebrain and computerbrain work together harmoniously.

Stop for a moment and consider some of the things in life that work for you. Perhaps you are a good parent. Have you ever asked yourself why? Have you ever tried to determine what it is that you do that makes your relationship with your children work as well as it does? Have you ever compared it with other relationships that don't work so well and considered what you do differently in those? Is it your attempt to communicate? Your ability to listen? Your willingness to be compassionate and understanding?

Perhaps you are an efficient administrator and have excellent organizational skills. Have you ever considered why your performance is so effective? Is it simply because you love your work? Is it because you are always dedicated to achieving your objectives? Or is it because you have the kind of corporate vision that enables you to see what needs to be done more clearly than those around you?

You may conclude that the things you do well you just do. You probably give no thought to or have any conscious awareness of why you succeed in these areas. You simply respond to the specific situation you were placed in.

THE SELF-BETTERMENT MOTIVE DETHRONED BY THE CAVEBRAIN

I want you to recognize not only what works for you, but also how you unfairly discount the achievements in emotional intelligence that have brought you your success.

So, if you consider yourself to be a good parent, you accept that categorically and proceed from there. If you are an efficient administrator, that too merely becomes a fact. When things go well there is very little to challenge you. It's in the new challenges we face, and especially when things go wrong, that the positive attributes from other areas will not necessarily assist you when you are wrestling with a new problem. In other words, these positive attributes are not always readily transferable.

Whatever it is you do well, those competencies prove that your computerbrain gives you tremendous power and control. When you react from your cavebrain, the opposite occurs: you temporarily block out the computerbrain, and the very attributes you need to create a smooth and harmonious flow are suppressed and no longer function as they should.

The cavebrain dethrones the self-betterment motive. I have spoken to unemployed executives whose current position, along with their advancing years, have caused them to feel extraordinarily insecure. Some are so devastated by their situation that they become manacled to their increasing negative self-perceptions. Fearful that they may never find a suitable job, they stagnate in negativity, convincing themselves of their inadequacies. With the idea of inadequacy and uselessness firmly imbedded in their minds they end up presenting themselves ineffectively at interviews. Some don't even bother to make a consistent effort after a spate of rejections. Some remain unemployed for months, even years. Others accept positions that severely underutilize their talents and skills—all because their emotions and subsequent cavebrain responses dethroned their computerbrain capacities.

What happened to the skills these people must have exhibited in their former high-power positions? Granted, there may have been a weak area somewhere in their mix of skills, but their strengths are still active. Such strengths serve self-betterment effectively. But they are quickly discounted and dismissed when emotional reactions undermine rational thinking and we become entrenched in the belief that we know why something is not going to work.

Somehow, however, we maintain our hope for self-betterment. We want life to work out better for ourselves. We know that it can. We only hope that we can make it without suffering through the murky pressures and daily frustrations that accompany the tyranny of the cavebrain. Unfortunately, the cavebrain gives us one major obstacle to that hoped-for state of harmony and power: stress. Dealing with it is key to our natural process of self-betterment.

Journal Entry

Man
Controlled by habit
Ruled by emotion
Placed by society rule
Dishonest by cynicism
Governed by creed
Determined to be freed
From behind the invisible bars

3

STRESS: EMOTIONAL CANCER

Excessive stress is emotional cancer. It destroys you from the inside out. It uses the emergency-response capacity of your cavebrain to maintain an unyielding state of physical and mental tension that eventually drains you of energy and equilibrium.

Stress becomes debilitating when the cavebrain is overloaded with perceived emergencies. It gets frazzled. The cavebrain is a high-voltage, short-duration mental tool. It is not designed to function continuously over time. High-voltage stress over long periods progressively blows the cavebrain's circuit capacity.

CONFUSION AT THE TOP OF THE FOOD CHAIN

Human beings rarely need to engage the fight-or-flight response associated with day-to-day physical survival. Nevertheless, we have maintained these automatic responses to perceived danger for thousands of years.

The momentum of thousands of years of cavebrain thinking and reacting programs us to handle all emergencies the same way: we react intensely for a brief period until the danger has passed. Unfortunately, interpersonal challenges are seldom short-term challenges; they are usually long-term, and the cavebrain, which is programmed to react quickly to emergencies, is not designed to handle sustained challenges. Immediate reaction and self-preservation is the cavebrain's goal.

Your interpersonal interactions demand more than reactive responses; they demand deeper thought, deeper consideration, and problem solving. They demand logical computerbrain responses, and considering alternatives takes time, as does understanding how to use the computerbrain to make positive, life-affirming decisions. Without training ourselves to process interpersonal challenges through the computerbrain, we allow our cavebrains to take control, which, ironically, creates the conditions where we ultimately lose control.

THE STRESS ATTACK

When your boss accidentally knocks over a coffee cup and the hot coffee spills towards you, your cavebrain leaps into action and you pull back immediately before thought intervenes. There it is: an instant self-preservation event. But when your project has been re-assigned and your boss begins dropping an ever-increasing volume of unreasonable demands upon you, your cavebrain's self-preservation motive kicks in and urges you to take action—to fight the situation, defend it, or avoid it. However, because your boss appears to have power over you, you perceive no immediate way out but to try to comply. Meanwhile, as your dissatisfaction mounts, your cavebrain continues to urge you to take action to rid yourself of the stinging pain of rejection and your mounting frustration. This is your cavebrain's reaction to an interpersonal attack.

Consider another scenario: you are on a fixed salary and a tight budget and you're near your limit on your credit cards. Your car breaks down and you've got to dig into your savings to pay for the repairs. You are angry and you verbally attack the mechanic, focusing all your frustrations on him, but you soon get over your anger—after all, what's the point?—and pay to get the car fixed. After a lousy day you come home. Your brother phones to tell you that he has lost his job and needs to borrow some money to pay his rent for the next couple of months. You feel an instant protective instinct mixed in with guilt, so you help him out. But you worry whether you can handle any more financial burdens. Suddenly your job security is in jeopardy. There are rumours of imminent lay-offs. You hear that your company intends to cut more than a thousand jobs. The newspapers are full of reports of similar things happening at other companies. You are unable to sleep at night, and you find yourself in a sustained stress situation.

In each of the above scenarios, you say to yourself, "I can't handle this." And you are right, in a way. The cavebrain cannot, and should not, be expected to work on its own to eliminate stress. This is the domain of the computerbrain. But if you have never been taught how to integrate higher thought into perceived emergencies, you short-circuit your own hard wiring and create more trouble than you ever anticipated.

So what happens when short-term stresses that you can handle become long-term stresses that you can't handle? Your brain copes with your emotional concerns in the same way it would if you were being attacked by a snake. You move yourself away from the danger or you attack it and try to eliminate the threat. You have the power to place yourself in a state of self-imposed terror. You are so terrified, so emotionally involved and sensitized that you continue operating from the standpoint of the cavebrain.

Something's got to give, and it usually does. Tensions with your boss or your spouse or your kids become confrontations, arguments, fights and, ultimately, severed relationships. Or your personal cash-flow problems become financial panics that lead you to make rash decisions you often end up regretting. Or worse, you weather the storm, which ultimately subsides on its own, leaving you no more informed or more skilled than before. Each time you face the situation, you simply repeat the cycle, and as this painful cycle continues, your self-confidence is slowly transformed into self-doubt. You develop low self-esteem and your life begins to move towards an unpleasant outcome.

The trouble is, while distressing emotional events do pass, their impact and emotional meaning linger, so the modern brain interprets these persistent messages as an incessant type of danger or pain. This is the emotional cancer: your self-protective system can become, in the end, a self-destructive system.

I am reminded of a tale by Heather Forest.

As two Zen monks walked along a muddy, rain-drenched road they came upon a lovely woman attempting to cross a large mud puddle. The elder monk stopped beside the woman, lifted her in his arms, and carried her across the puddle. He set her gently down on the dry ridge of the road as the younger monk discreetly admired her charms.

After bowing politely to the woman, the two monks continued down the muddy road. The younger monk was sullen and silent as they walked along. They travelled over the hills, down around the valleys, through a town, and under forest trees. At last, after many hours had passed, the younger monk scolded the elder, "You are aware that we monks do not touch women! Why did you carry that girl?"

The elder monk slowly turned and smiled. He said, "My dear young brother, you have such heavy thoughts! I left the woman alongside the road hours ago. Why are you still carrying her?"

THE EMOTIONAL DERAILMENT OF PAIN

None of us will likely forget the terrifying devastation of the 1995 Oklahoma City bombing that killed 168 people. The emotional shock of the event touched millions of people around the world. It touched those who lost loved ones in the explosion, and it touched the rescuers at the scene in perhaps a more profound way than any of us could imagine.

Terry Yeakey, an Oklahoma City police officer, pulled three men and one woman from the crumbled remains of the Alfred P. Murrah Federal Building, saving their lives. This wasn't Yeakey's first involvement with mass death. In 1990, he served in the Persian Gulf War where his duties included taking part in the mass burials of Iraqi civilians killed during the conflict.

Yeakey, whose passion in life was educating schoolchildren about drug abuse, had a tremendously strong survival motive. Despite the four lives he saved on that April afternoon in 1995, Yeakey was distraught because he had suffered a two-storey fall through a hole in the building following his rescue of the four victims. He wasn't upset about his own injuries from the fall. He was upset because the back injury he sustained as a result of the fall prevented him from continuing the rescue. According to his mother, Terry said, "Had I not fallen, I could have saved more lives."

The emotions of the event haunted him. On May 7, 1996, four days before he was to be awarded the medal of honour for his bravery, Terry Yeakey took his own life. He was emotionally devastated by the killings and deaths he was powerless to prevent. He had no faith that psychiatric counselling would help him, and he was unable to find a balance of emotion and understanding that would allow him to regain his essential sense of self-worth and manage the profound stresses of guilt and powerlessness that plagued him.

Few of us will ever face such horrifying events as Terry Yeakey faced— events that shake our emotional intelligence out of alignment very quickly and very dramatically. Nevertheless, the stresses we face can be equally insidious, leaving our powerful emotional reactions unsupported and robbing us of the critically valuable input of our reasoning capacity.

THE MISDIRECTED COMPUTERBRAIN

Stress is, basically, the designation of the right assignment to the wrong part of your brain, all because the emotional trigger in the assignment has you reacting in a self-preservation mode instead of a self-reflection mode. As mentioned earlier, modern life presents us with few situations that require the cavebrain's self-preserving approach.

Identifying legitimate instant emotions like anger, fear, resentment, or pity gives you the notion that you are handling them. Identifying them, however, is far simpler than resolving them. When you allow the emotional input to build and build until it reaches a sustained level, your capacity to identify and reflect on your emotions doesn't help you very much. Your reactions don't lead to solutions because solutions to ongoing problems are processed by the neocortex/computerbrain, not the amygdala/cavebrain, and you have not yet effectively engaged the computerbrain.

Our reactions, however, continue to trigger the cavebrain, and these reactions force you into a prototypical fight-or-flight reaction mode. You don't know how to find the solution because you have never been trained or encouraged to isolate and understand the emotion in the first place.

DEBILITATING REACTIONS TO ARTIFICIAL STRESS

We are not the only ones who initiate the cycle that leads to internal stress.

Consider the horrors we invite into our brains through the media: radio news, TV news, newspapers, magazines, the Internet, and the like. Media corporations know how to manufacture, manipulate, and induce our levels of stress by proxy. They pummel us with reports that are increasingly presented as life-or-death issues that affect us all. These reports are presented dramatically, so as to gain your cavebrain attention, prompting you to feel an instant emotion that bypasses the logic of your computerbrain. Television news, for example, grabs you at the cavebrain level in order to hopefully keep you glued to the set, thus increasing viewer ratings, keeping you watching the program through the commercials, and ultimately increasing advertising revenues.

Meanwhile, what is going on in your brain? Your cavebrain is initiating its fight-or-flight mode to help you survive the imminent danger you have just identified. But how imminent is this danger, really? Is it imminent at all? How many of these dangers truly affect you? Few. But in our highly controlled and predictable world we actually enjoy feeling emotion whenever and wherever we can get it, even if it's force-fed to us. We want emotion. We want to feel.

The trouble is, such emotions, when presented in this fashion, are in essence illegitimate. We take them in but then we have no way to process them. The emotions linger, the cavebrain's "on" mode continues, and eventually our capacity to distinguish between genuine emotions and force-fed emotions diminishes. Today we hear reports of an escalating number of children becoming killers. What is most disturbing about this trend is that these juvenile killers are increasingly emerging from society's mainstream. For many, there is nothing unusual about their lives, no way to predict an impending tragedy. They are the kids next door. They live what seem to be uneventful, normal lives. They deal with the same stresses as everyone. The difference is that the sustained stresses they face have become more and more intense. The distinguishing predictive feature is harder to isolate but it is there. That feature is the child's capacity to handle the barrage of artificially created stresses. When that capacity is exceeded, even the mildest stress can lead to destruction and self-destruction.

CAUGHT IN THE HEADLIGHTS

When you consider this barrage of stresses, it is not surprising that so many of us have difficulty with self-confidence or self-esteem. When self-esteem is not intact or self-esteem is bruised, a form of emotional paralysis occurs. When you are caught in a situation heavily laden with negative stimuli you remain paralyzed by inaction, much in the way a deer stands paralyzed in the glare of oncoming headlights. It cannot move itself out of harm's way.

Through lack of self-confidence or self-esteem or the inability or refusal to take responsibility, you tend to experience the same kind of inaction. You suppress making any decisions about the stressful emotional situations confronting you. You believe that if you do nothing, then nothing further will go wrong. But as we all know, bad situations have a tendency to get worse. Under such conditions, you are afraid to take responsibility for productive change. Your emotions paralyze you and discourage action. Why? Because your cavebrain is in total survival mode. It is instantly attempting to maintain whatever level of stability it can. And when you are unaware that this is what you are doing, you don't have the opportunity to begin integrating your rational (computerbrain) capacities with your emotional capacities. Inaction merely causes a mental burden and further pain.

Think of a situation that troubles you enormously. Ask yourself why you feel you cannot manage the situation as effectively as you would like to. You will probably conclude that your emotions are getting in the way. With emotions like guilt, fear, shame, or anger dominating your thought process, any or all of these emotions will sabotage the balance between logic and emotion.

Once there is insufficient logical consideration, you will struggle with the dilemma through lack of confidence and reliable information. Increasingly, you will find yourself in pure cavebrain mode. With your cavebrain reactions acting without the natural balancing input of your computerbrain, you further compromise your position by not clearly defining and understanding your objective. This distortion will likely result in an avoidance response. Without a natural balance between the legitimate survival motive of your cavebrain and the essential rational input of your computerbrain, the stress of being unable to achieve your goals is frequently debilitating.

Sustained stresses take their toll on all of us. They overwork the cavebrain and steadily diminish our inner fire. You know what it feels like. You become less excited about the good things in life and more complacent about the dangers in life. You lose the full dynamism of being human because stress has become dominant in your life.

THE INSTITUTIONALIZATION OF THE
SELF-BETTERMENT MOTIVE

Our cavebrain enabled us not only to avoid danger but to hunt our prey so we could eat. Our hunting skills evolved, and we learned how to domesticate our prey. Our lives became easier and easier.

Today, the pressure to succeed and improve is so intense that even when you're busy bettering yourself, you're never quite measuring up to society's standards. It's easy to feel out-maneuvered and out-performed. Our culture keeps raising the standards so quickly and so high, we frequently perceive that we are not keeping up. What is happening? We have institutionalized the human self-betterment motive. It has warped the realm of evolutionary improvement prompted by our immediate life needs and has become an all-consuming personal demand to attain more, more, more. It would be as if in our cave days, we were expected to hunt down one woolly mammoth every day instead of every two months. The cave-brain is asked to sustain an intensity that it is unable to sustain, and in the end, stress, stress, and more stress.

THE KEY TO COPING

Most of us don't deal with stress very well because we don't fully understand its source. Therefore, we don't know how to keep it from dominating and controlling us, and many of us certainly don't know how to recognize it when it attacks us, let alone relieve it when it grips us.

The usual coping mechanism: we carry on mumbling and muttering away until the stress seems to subside, like a windstorm. Or worse, we try to numb the pain of stress with alcohol or drugs. Unfortunately, the stress has already done its damage. We are usually in the middle of a new source of stress before we have had the opportunity to deal with the current stress, and the scenario will repeat itself soon, and again and again.

Journal Entry

All one, alone
I want a balance in my life,
a balance to deal with
Hurt
Happiness
Sorrow
Success
Love
Parenthood
Feelings

Friends
Hope
Religion
Marriage
Strength
Weakness
And above all
I want a balance in
my acceptance that
I must take responsibility

4

INTERNALIZATION: THE INVISIBLE BARS THAT ENTRAP YOU

When we are functioning well, we have the capacity to deal with problems in a balanced, well-managed way; we have the capacity to manage situations logically and appropriately. When we are functioning well, we reflect on issues quietly and allow our computerbrain to function unhindered. If there is a sense of frustration, resentment, or anger, we handle the emotion effectively.

Our capacity to be angry, fearful, happy, content, logical, wise, and analytical relies on our ability to harmonize and manage our emotions. When one emotion monopolizes the consciousness, you do not approach the situation in a balanced cavebrain-computerbrain way, thus allowing your cavebrain to quickly take charge. But there is another aspect of human emotional response that we cannot ignore: internalization.

A NATURAL INSTINCT OF SURVIVAL

Internalization at normal levels is one of nature's ways of providing self-protection. It is an alternative to the two most common emotional survival reactions: fight or flight. Internalization is the third option: withdrawing from a situation. When it is functioning correctly, the process of withdrawing allows you to evade dangerous confrontations, provides you with privacy, gives you the time to reflect and engage the computerbrain to solve problems, and allows you to plan what action you want to take and how to engage those actions.

It is sometimes difficult to recognize how this primal reaction operates in humans. Observe how it works in the animal kingdom, and you can see how natural it is. Picture this scene: it is a bright winter's day, and virgin snow covers the valley like a soft carpet. Suddenly this tranquil scene is disrupted by a spray of powdery snow as a rabbit bursts into the open from a thicket, fleeing from a fox that has been chasing it. The rabbit darts forward through the snow, completely exposed. Just then, the fox zigzags into the field, frantically sniffing the ground and air, and darting from one place to another trying to pick up the rabbit's scent. The rabbit sees the fox, and with nowhere to hide, it suddenly stops, frozen with fright. Fortunately, the wind carries the rabbit's scent away from the fox and its stillness hides it completely. The fox continues its search, but with no helpful clues as to the whereabouts of its prey, it soon abandons the hunt and heads in another direction. Just as quickly, the rabbit moves into the sanctuary of the undergrowth.

Nature has its own wonderful way of ensuring survival. The rabbit's reaction wasn't either fight or flight—the two most common primal reactions. Fighting was obviously not an option. Nor was fleeing. After all, if the rabbit had decided to make a run for it, the fox would have spotted it in an instant and hunted it down. So the rabbit chose a third option: it froze. Non-action in this case saved the rabbit's life.

Complete non-activity is one of nature's alternatives that provides a period of safety long enough to generate other options. Non-action is one of nature's most effective emotional reactions to a perceived threat. The rabbit's stillness dramatically reduced its foe's ability to identify its whereabouts. Humans use a similar method when they feel overwhelmed— internalization.

Internalization is the process of initially deciding not to act upon emotions in the belief that taking action will make matters worse. Like everything in life, moderation in the use of internalization is essential to unified cavebrain-computerbrain functioning. Avoiding dangerous confrontations is wise. But even more often, we mistake interactions and important confrontations for dangerous confrontations, and react to them the same way: by internalizing. This is when trouble begins. For some people, withdrawing from situations completely becomes their automatic method of dealing with unpleasant situations, and the inertia caused by unwarranted withdrawl creates a negative cycle of stagnation. This approach constitutes excessive internalization.

PROTECTING YOURSELF FROM MISPERCEIVED DANGERS

Excessive internalization takes the healthy process of withdrawing to an unhealthy extreme. This level of internalization appears to protect you. The options provided by your emotional reactions of fight-or-flight don't present themselves as viable. Excessive discomfort or fear forces you to overinternalize. You fear that by engaging emotionally charged interactions, you will make matters worse and jeopardize your position. This fear of engagement is far more powerful than the fear of failure or defeat, so by excessively internalizing you hide your reactions and try to numb your emotion. You become stagnant, hoping that the situation will just disappear. You are not thinking rationally. Rational thought is just about the last thing going on.

Consider a student of mine: Harris is an intelligent and kind man, but highly withdrawn. We remained in contact many years after he completed Witz Training sessions on effective communication and emotional management. After one of the first classes he attended, it was apparent that he was not clear about some aspects of the session. I noticed through his posture and lack of participation that he was uncomfortable with the experience. I asked him if he had any questions. After much encouragement, he opened up a little: "Well, ah, yes, I think that I've got lots of questions, but I don't want you to think I'm stupid or something." With this comment he started to feel resentful. His resentment was now focused on me, and I became the visible source of his discomfort.

Harris took the training course in order to address the discomfort he felt in emotionally charged situations. However, his fear of being judged or put down dominated him in his discussion with me. Thus, his overriding compulsion was to remain silent, and the stress of wanting—and not wanting—his discomfort to be addressed made him angry. Suddenly, all of the negative emotions he normally experienced came rushing in and his instinct was to remain inert both physically and intellectually, but not emotionally. Harris and many others in this predicament rely on heavy internalization in the face of emotional discomfort.

The typical flow of events when you overinternalize are as follows: You launch an internal dialogue which is usually negative self-talk. This allows you to arrive at all manner of conclusions—usually negative—and with the state of non-action, you quickly become overwhelmed by the ever-increasing enormity of your problem. Once this occurs, fear of just about everything ensures that you remain paralyzed by your emotions. With only your fears as a reference point, nothing changes.

I have observed many such overinternalizations, and have noticed that, typically, a highly withdrawn person will attempt to convince you that there is no problem at all and that everything is fine. Beneath the individual's façade, however, just the opposite is occurring. Moreover, highly withdrawn individuals will blame the source of their feelings on someone other than themselves.

When I began working with Harris, I was amazed at how quickly he would blame his discomfort and perceived inabilities on everyone else. He would say things like, "He made me feel . . ." or he would state his own opinion as if it were fact. In one instance, he manufactured an entire conversation in his head and concluded facts that at no time invited comment or validation from the other party. In fact, the other party was oblivious to any problem. Manufactured realities become a major recurring factor when you are in a highly withdrawn state. With nothing to go on other than imagination, you can, and often do, create larger problems for yourself. Imagination has no logical restrictions or boundaries, and in the absence of effectively integrated computerbrain activity, emotions run amok, free to create any truth they desire.

PAIN IN THE PRISON OF YOUR MIND

Excessive internalization has the power to dominate the personality. Even if you are not prone to excessive internalization, you can still find yourself overinternalizing. Certain situations or personalities prompt you to withdraw, making it very difficult for you to manage important areas in your life. Internalization doesn't eliminate your source of stress; it simply re-creates the struggle within yourself. And because internalization on its own achieves no resolutions, it must, by definition, become sustained inaction, which prevents you from grabbing hold of and dealing with your concerns. Any emotion that drives you to withdraw becomes so all-consuming that you do not test the validity of your conclusions, so you remain more entrenched in inaction. With the visualization of the danger or extreme discomfort uppermost in your mind, you quickly become fixated on the most benign aspects of your problem. You follow cycles of thought that don't connect to any action of an interpersonal, physical, or intellectual nature. Your mind spins endlessly around the same emotional quandaries and pushes out everything else.

The effects of internalization are debilitating. Your attempts to become invisible leave you rigid and frozen. You stagnate. You feel an overwhelming desire to do nothing. You are paralyzed, unable to engage and address the issues most important to you. Not surprisingly, you feel resentful, frustrated, and unhappy. Worst of all, you diminish your capacity to integrate the cavebrain and computerbrain. At no time is it more important to engage your computerbrain capacity and take action than when you are suffering the effects of excessive internalization.

Recognizing that there is a way out is the first step towards addressing and managing excessive internalization. The second step is to know yourself better.

LOOKING AT YOURSELF OBJECTIVELY

Our goal must be to integrate the self-preserving motive of our cavebrain with the problem-solving capacity of our computerbrain. We need to present the data we are processing in our brains to the rational, logical mind. You are equipped right now with the tools to distinguish between the need for cavebrain reactions and the need for computerbrain actions. For most of us, however, these tools only operate in the most ideal conditions. They function in us not as a reliable system but as a grace bestowed upon us from time to time.

Until now you have had no way of formally educating and training yourself to deal with your emotions. Read on. This book will teach you a powerful way to achieve the smooth integration of the cavebrain and computerbrain. The first step to handling the cavebrain's incessant reign of error and terror is to recognize and identify and test the extent to which you are being ruled by your cavebrain and in what specific areas of life you are affected most. So, get out your pencil and prepare to take the emotional intelligence test.

Journal Entry

Change is a perpetual motion.

5

THE EMOTIONAL INTELLIGENCE TEST

Emotional intelligence is not a single, distinct human capacity. It is a fluid, dynamic capacity that reflects an ongoing ability to integrate your computerbrain's rational capacities with your cavebrain's critically important emotional input. Emotional intelligence can both decrease and increase in effectiveness. It can be influenced both by issues and events surrounding you and by your own efforts to efficiently integrate intelligence with emotion.

Each of us tends to think that our emotions are unique. It's true that what caused your emotions initially may have been a unique event. It is also true, however, that your level of emotional intelligence will likely follow established patterns. So, what you tend to do with your system of emotion and reasoning is predictable and measurable. These patterns determine your emotional intelligence.

Unlike traditional IQ measurements, emotional intelligence (EQ) is one capacity that you can actually control and raise to any level you wish. There are no limits. It has one consistent goal: to achieve a balance between emotion and intellect. When you integrate the way you feel with the way you think, your potential for fulfillment is limitless. It is this objective that each of us needs to strive for and maintain.

Because EQ is dynamic, it is more difficult to quantify than IQ. This chapter will help you measure emotional intelligence in order to give you an accurate picture of how effectively you are integrating your cavebrain reactions with your computerbrain response, and how your level of cavebrain-computerbrain integration has affected your level of self-esteem. (See chapter 6 for emotional intelligence test interpretations.)

THE WITZ TRAINING PROGRAM ASSESSMENT

The questions that comprise this five-section test are derived from the comprehensive assessment completed by each participant in the Witz Training programs.

The test has been abridged so that you can focus on your core emotional management skills. It will allow you to evaluate:

- how dominant your cavebrain reactions are in your daily life;
- how powerful your computerbrain's reasoning capacity is in your daily life;
- how you direct your emotions; and
- how your current level of self-esteem reflects your ability to integrate your computerbrain reasoning with your cavebrain reactions.

HOW TO COMPLETE YOUR ASSESSMENT

Sections 1, 2, 3, and 4 each include a series of 15 questions. Each of these series of questions is designed to measure a unique aspect of your cavebrain, computerbrain, and emotion channeling capacities. Section 5 is a 25-question assessment that evaluates your self-esteem in relation to your cavebrain, computerbrain, and emotion channeling capacities.

The test questions will take about half an hour to complete.

You will notice score letters and boxes situated to the right side of each question. They will enable you to accurately add up specific categorical scores at the end of the assessment. As you answer your questions, you don't need to know what these category score letters mean. At this point just circle the number that best answers each question, then write that number in the box. Don't worry about the accompanying score letters.

Example Question

I'd like to hear your point of view.

1 2 3 4 5   C=☐

Assessment Section I

How to Answer the Questions

Read the questions in Section 1. Look at the type of words in each statement and their nature rather than the exact words.

For each question, ask yourself how often you use thoughts or words or statements similar to those listed. Then circle the appropriate number between 1 and 5 that most accurately defines the frequency with which you use each statement in your day-to-day life.

The numbers represent the following frequencies:

1 Never/Very Rarely

2 Seldom

3 Occasionally

4 Very Frequently

5 Always

Example Question

Here is a question from Section 1:

I'd rather not talk about it.

1 2 3 4 5 E= ☐

As you consider this question, think about what the statement says. For example, you may not say this exact phrase or even think it using these exact words, but it may be a genuine inner response nonetheless. In other words, you may think or say something like, "I don't want to talk about it," or "Let's not go there," or "I don't feel comfortable talking about this."

Now, once you have determined that the meaning behind the statement is something that you understand and appreciate, go to the frequency rating numbers and decide how frequently you find yourself thinking or speaking these thoughts. If, for example, you rarely hold back from expressing your opinions about things, even highly sensitive issues, and you have no trouble thinking or speaking about them, circle the number 1. This would indicate that you never or very rarely steer clear of such interactions. On the other hand, if you find that people are asking you about things or that you are constantly faced with topics and situations that are uncomfortable for you to think or speak about, circle 5. This indicates that you always would rather not talk about such topics. You may fall in the middle with certain subjects. In these cases, consider selecting the "Seldom" option (2), or the "Occasional" option (3).

You should now have a clear idea about how to complete the assessments.

Please begin now with Section 1.

Section 1 Assessment Questions

1. I hate your guts!

   1 2 3 4 5 F= ☐

2. I'm sorry.

   1 2 3 4 5 E= ☐

3. I'd like to hear your point of view.

   1 2 3 4 5 C= ☐

4. I don't give a damn.

   1 2 3 4 5 F= ☐

5. People really don't care.

   1 2 3 4 5 E= ☐

6. Is there more information you could provide me with?

   1 2 3 4 5 C= ☐

7. I'd rather not talk about it.

   1 2 3 4 5 E= ☐

8. What are the pros and cons?

   1 2 3 4 5 C= ☐

9. F**k you. (The use of foul language.)

1 2 3 4 5   F= ☐

10. I wonder what caused this?

1 2 3 4 5   C= ☐

11. Get the hell out of here!

1 2 3 4 5   F= ☐

12. Remaining silent with discomfort.

1 2 3 4 5   E= ☐

13. Let's look at this logically. . .

1 2 3 4 5   C= ☐

14. Get off my back.

1 2 3 4 5   F= ☐

15. I'm afraid.

1 2 3 4 5   E= ☐

Totalling Your Scores in Section 1

This is the end of Assessment Section 1. Now add up all your scores that correspond to the individual C, E, and F category scores. For example, questions 3, 5, 7, 8, and 13 are C questions. Add up the total scores for those five questions and place that single number in the box titled C. Do the same with your E and F scores.

F ☐   C ☐   E ☐

Please continue now with Assessment Section 2.

Assessment Section 2

How to Answer the Questions

Read the descriptions in Section 2. For each of the following descriptions ask yourself how frequently you find yourself using each verbal or non-verbal form of communication. Then circle the appropriate number between 1 and 5 that most accurately defines the frequency with which you use each one in your day-to-day life.

The numbers represent the following frequencies:

1 Never/Very Rarely

2 Seldom

3 Occasionally

4 Very Frequently

5 Always

Section 2 Assessment Questions

1. Talking very softly, almost mumbling.

   1 2 3 4 5   E= ☐

2. Maintaining regular eye contact while you are talking.

   1 2 3 4 5   C= ☐

3. Angrily shouting instead of talking.

   1 2 3 4 5   F= ☐

4. Tearful.

   1 2 3 4 5   E= ☐

5. Talking at the right pace, neither too fast nor too slow.

   1 2 3 4 5   C= ☐

6. Difficulty in maintaining eye contact.

   1 2 3 4 5   E= ☐

7. Angrily protesting.

    1 2 3 4 5 F= ☐

8. Using a simpering or whining tone of voice.

    1 2 3 4 5 E= ☐

9. Using an indignant, angry tone of voice.

    1 2 3 4 5 F= ☐

10. Using a well-modulated voice.

    1 2 3 4 5 C= ☐

11. Keeping eye contact to a minimum.

    1 2 3 4 5 E= ☐

12. Using an appropriate amount of emphasis (not too much, nor too little).

    1 2 3 4 5 C= ☐

13. Using a tense, uptight tone of voice.

    1 2 3 4 5 F= ☐

14. Maintaining a relaxed, confident stance.

    1 2 3 4 5 C= ☐

15. Using aggressive or threatening movement to emphasize feelings.

    1 2 3 4 5 F= ☐

Totalling Your Scores in Section 2

This is the end of Assessment Section 2. Now add up all your scores that correspond to the individual C, E, and F category scores for Section 2 only, just as you did in Section 1.

F ☐   C ☐   E ☐

Please continue now with Assessment Section 3.

Assessment Section 3

How to Answer the Questions

Read the statements in Section 3. For each statement ask yourself how often you feel each one applies to you. Then circle the appropriate number between 1 and 5 that most accurately defines the frequency with which each one applies to your day-to-day life.

The numbers represent the following frequencies:

1 Never/Very Rarely

2 Seldom

3 Occasionally

4 Very Frequently

5 Always

Section 3 Assessment Questions

1. I am analytical.
    1 2 3 4 5 C= ☐

2. I am angry.
    1 2 3 4 5 F= ☐

3. I am lonely.
    1 2 3 4 5 E= ☐

4. I am often aggressive (be it verbally or physically).
    1 2 3 4 5 F= ☐

5. I am not impulsive.
    1 2 3 4 5 C= ☐

6. I tend to sulk.
    1 2 3 4 5 E= ☐

7. I am rebellious.

    1 2 3 4 5 F= ☐

8. I tend to avoid aggressive people.

    1 2 3 4 5 E= ☐

9. I am conceited.

    1 2 3 4 5 F= ☐

10. I have a tendency to withdraw from situations which I find uncomfortable.

    1 2 3 4 5 E= ☐

11. I am decisive.

    1 2 3 4 5 C= ☐

12. I am stubborn.

    1 2 3 4 5 F= ☐

13. I am logical.

    1 2 3 4 5 C= ☐

14. I am a procrastinator.

    1 2 3 4 5 E= ☐

15. I am rational.

    1 2 3 4 5 C= ☐

Totalling Your Scores in Section 3

This is the end of Assessment Section 3. Now add up all your scores that correspond to the individual C, E, and F category scores for Section 3 only.

F ☐   C ☐   E ☐

Please continue now with Assessment Section 4.

Assessment Section 4

How to Answer the Questions

Read the statements in Section 4. For each statement ask yourself how often you feel each one applies to you. Then circle the appropriate number between 1 and 5 that most accurately defines the frequency with which each one applies to your day-to-day life.

The numbers represent the following frequencies:

1 Never/Very Rarely

2 Seldom

3 Occasionally

4 Very Frequently

5 Always

Section 4 Assessment Questions

1. I react angrily when confronted or criticized.

   1 2 3 4 5 F= ☐

2. At social gatherings, I tend to talk about work.

   1 2 3 4 5 C= ☐

3. I am very rational with my money, never splashing out impulsively.

   1 2 3 4 5 C= ☐

4. Swearing is appropriate if I can't get my point across.

   1 2 3 4 5 F= ☐

5. I tend to be overwhelmed by problems and find it difficult to make decisions.

   1 2 3 4 5 E= ☐

6. I believe knowledge is a contributor to success.

   1 2 3 4 5 C= ☐

7. I believe privacy is necessary and important.

   1 2 3 4 5 E= ☐

8. I belong or associate with professional groups whose prime objective is to exchange knowledge.

   1 2 3 4 5 C= ☐

9. I belong or associate with groups which are primarily opposed to existing authorities.

   1 2 3 4 5 F= ☐

10. I find it difficult to approach people.

    1 2 3 4 5 E= ☐

11. I believe in the right to rebel against rules.

    1 2 3 4 5 F= ☐

12. I believe everybody has the right to do what they want to do, regardless of the consequences.

    1 2 3 4 5 F= ☐

13. I often put off starting things I know I should do.

    1 2 3 4 5 E= ☐

14. My closest friends are limited to my business associates.

    1 2 3 4 5 C= ☐

15. I tend to say "I can't" when I really mean "I won't" or "I don't want to."

    1 2 3 4 5 E= ☐

Totalling Your Scores in Section 4

This is the end of Assessment Section 4. Now add up all your scores that correspond to the individual C, E, and F category scores for Section 5 only.

F ☐   C ☐   E ☐

Totalling All Your Categorical Assessment Scores

Now go to the end of each of the previous four test sections where you totalled your categorical scores for each question. Add the total for each unique category letter score for each question together with the same category letter score in Section 1, Section 2, Section 3, and Section 4. Place those final totals in the following boxes.

C ☐   E ☐   F ☐

Assessment Section 5

How to Answer the Questions

Read the questions in Section 5 and then circle the number between 0 and 4 that most accurately defines the frequency with which each statement applies to your day-to-day life. The numbers represent the following:

0   I disagree completely

1   I somewhat disagree

2   I slightly agree

3   I somewhat agree

4   I agree completely

The asterisks indicate questions of particular import which we will refer to and discuss in more detail later in the book. For now only place your answer in Box A.

Section 5 Assessment Questions

1. What matters most is that I believe in myself, not what others believe of me.

    0 1 2 3 4   A ☐   B ☐

2. The best way to get things done is to do them myself.

    0 1 2 3 4   A ☐   *   B ☐

3. It is difficult for me to admit when I am wrong.

    0 1 2 3 4   A ☐   *   B ☐

4. Not getting the recognition I deserve is a clear sign that others don't appreciate or understand my ideas.

    0 1 2 3 4   A ☐   *   B ☐

5. I feel that I can accomplish anything I put my mind to.

    0 1 2 3 4   A ☐   B ☐

6. I feel that I have the same opportunities that others have.

   0 1 2 3 4 A ☐   B ☐

7. Good things just don't seem to happen to me.

   0 1 2 3 4 A ☐ * B ☐

8. Those who speak up probably have better ideas than I do, so I tend to keep quiet.

   0 1 2 3 4 A ☐ * B ☐

9. I am usually accepting of other people's faults.

   0 1 2 3 4 A ☐   B ☐

10. I strongly defend my actions no matter what.

   0 1 2 3 4 A ☐ * B ☐

11. I don't focus on creating a good impression; who I truly am is good enough.

   0 1 2 3 4 A ☐   B ☐

12. I find it difficult to cope with losing or being wrong.

   0 1 2 3 4 A ☐ * B ☐

13. I never feel lost or out of place with new people.

   0 1 2 3 4 A ☐   B ☐

14. I find it difficult to make decisions and stick to them.

   0 1 2 3 4 A ☐ * B ☐

15. It is usually a bad idea to show your true emotions.

   0 1 2 3 4 A ☐ * B ☐

16. I try to always express myself, even if it means being judged by others.

   0 1 2 3 4 A ☐   B ☐

17. My relationship with others can be stormy and difficult to manage.

0 1 2 3 4   A ☐   *   B ☐

18. I cannot afford to take the risk of trying something new.

0 1 2 3 4   A ☐   *   B ☐

19. The potential for failure in this world far outweighs the potential for great success.

0 1 2 3 4   A ☐   *   B ☐

20. I am often suspicious of the intentions of others. Only a fool is trusting.

0 1 2 3 4   A ☐   *   B ☐

21. I adapt well to new situations.

0 1 2 3 4   A ☐   B ☐

22. I tend to become defensive when criticized or challenged.

0 1 2 3 4   A ☐   *   B ☐

23. I have no trouble being proud of the success of others.

0 1 2 3 4   A ☐   B ☐

24. I question the methods of high achievers.

0 1 2 3 4   A ☐   *   B ☐

25. I find it difficult to accept/believe the praise of others.

0 1 2 3 4   A ☐   *   B ☐

This is the end of Assessment Section 5, and the end of the emotional intelligence test.

This score relates to the scores you achieved in Sections 1, 2, 3, and 4.

Totalling Your Scores in Section 5

Totalling your scores in Section 5 is a little different than for Sections 1 through 4. It is a four-step process that will take you a couple of minutes. Here is what you do.

Step 1

Transfer the scores in column A to the box directly beside it in column B. However, do not transfer the column A scores that have an asterisk (*) between column A and B.

Step 2

Now locate the scores from the questions with an asterisk (*) between the columns. Take the individual score for each of these questions and, one at a time, re-score the answers according to the table below, and place the transposed score to the box directly beside it in column B. The table is an exact transposition of the scores as originally written beside each question. A good way to remember if you have transposed the scores properly is to make sure that when you add up your original score with the transposed score, it always adds up to 4.

Original score		Converted score
0	→	4
1	→	3
2	→	2
3	→	1
4	→	0

Here, for example, is how you might re-score the results for the first six questions according to the table above.

1. What matters most is that I believe in myself, not what others believe of me.

    0 1 2 3 4   A $\boxed{1}$ *   B $\boxed{3}$

Note: When A score is transposed, the score of 1 becomes a score of 3, and $1 + 3 = 4$.

2. The best way to get things done is to do them myself.

0 1 2 3 4   A$\boxed{2}$ *   B$\boxed{2}$

Note: When A score is transposed, it remains the same, and 2 + 2 = 4.

3. It is difficult for me to admit when I am wrong.

0 1 2 3 4   A$\boxed{0}$ *   B$\boxed{4}$

Note: When A score is transposed, the score of 1 becomes a score of 3, and 0 + 4 = 4.

Step 3

Add up all the scores of column B only.

Step 4

Place your Section 5 score in the following box.

$\boxed{}$

6

INTERPRETING YOUR EMOTIONAL INTELLIGENCE TEST RESULTS

Now that you have completed the emotional intelligence test it is time to define your level of emotional intelligence by examining your scores.

GETTING THE MOST FROM THE RESULTS

The results you get will not be a single-digit number such as in a traditional IQ test. Rather, your scores will define how closely your emotional intelligence pattern aligns with the ideal level of integrated emotion and reason. This chapter will help you interpret your results.

First you will find an explanation of the letter-score categorizations. Second, you will find the balanced scores that would be achieved by an emotionally intelligent individual. Next are interpretations of the most common emotional intelligence score pattern. The rest of the chapter is devoted to specific interpretations of each range of scores within each category: cavebrain, computerbrain, internalization, in addition to complete self-esteem analyses and interpretations.

Although you might want to begin reading the analyses and interpretations of your categorical scores which begin on page 68, please read the next few pages first. They will explain what the categories mean. They will tell you what the ideal emotional intelligence pattern scores are for each category. And they will show you what the various combinations of scores tell you about your current emotional intelligence level and how you can use these insights to get the most from the rest of the book.

APPRECIATING THE LIMITS OF PAPER-BASED TESTING

Although this chapter outlines a tremendous number of evaluations and interpretations that will give you important insights into your emotional intelligence, it gives you the most thorough evaluation of your emotional intelligence that you can arrive at through a paper-based test. Training course programs test in a more extended way and use a more individualistic approach. If the input from these extended assessments were to be incorporated, the number of combined evaluations would fill a number of volumes. Rest assured, however, that the results you gain from the interpretations contained in this chapter will help you accurately define your emotional intelligence or lack thereof.

Overall, any variation of score-pattern ranges from the ideal ranges outlined on pages 65–66 will be obvious in behaviours and levels of self-esteem that work against your own best interests and the interests of those around you.

I would also like to remind you that the exact levels of your cavebrain input, computerbrain input, and internalization varies from day to day. Nevertheless, you will probably achieve scores in each area that remain within a certain range over a long period of time, that is, until you begin to apply the new systems and strategies presented in this book.

EMOTIONAL INTELLIGENCE CATEGORIES
(WHAT THOSE SCORE LETTERS MEAN)

Test sections 1, 2, 3, and 4 each included category score letters for each question. Here is what they referred to.

F-category scores This is your cavebrain score. It measures your current active levels of primal emotion.

C-category scores This is your computerbrain score. It is not an IQ test that measures how smart you are; rather, it measures your current active capacity to apply your rational reasoning.

E-category scores This is your internalization score. It measures whether you process your cavebrain reactions as outward behaviour that primarily affects others or as inward behaviour that primarily affects yourself.

Test section 5 was the Self-Esteem Assessment. It did not include any category score letters. This is because the Self-Esteem Assessment is a stand-alone assessment that gives you a single benchmark from which to evaluate the categorical scores in sections 1 though 4.

COMPOSITE PROFILE OF THE EMOTIONALLY INTELLIGENT INDIVIDUAL

The following scores provide a composite profile of what an emotionally intelligent individual feels, thinks, and does.

These scores should not be interpreted in isolation. They work interdependently, and they depend on your self-esteem score. I discovered a long time ago that the basic building material for healthy emotional intelligence is stable self-esteem. There is an established link between self-esteem and rational thought. The one supports the other.

Following are the collective individual category scores which, when combined as described below, comprise the profile of the emotionally intelligent individual:

Ideal Cavebrain (F) Score: 33–35

Your level of primal cavebrain (amygdala) emotions is strong enough to allow you to be fully in touch with them and for them to be meaningful and influential in your life. But this level is not so intense that it prevents you from integrating computerbrain input into your thinking and decisions.

(See your actual score interpretations beginning on page 68.)

Ideal Computerbrain (C) Score: 79–82

Your computerbrain (neocortex) reasoning capacity is strong enough to enable you to analyze and interpret feedback and use it to arrive at reasonable solutions, but it is not so active that you overanalyze input to the extent that you don't arrive at solutions when you should.

(See your actual score interpretations beginning on page 70.)

Ideal Internalization (E) Score: 23–35

Your internalization score is high enough that you are able to work through your strong emotions on your own, but low enough that you are able to express your emotions in a healthy and productive manner.

(See your actual score interpretations beginning on page 73.)

Ideal Self-Esteem Score: 76–82

Your self-esteem reflects how well your emotional intelligence is working. This is an ideal self-esteem score and must be balanced with other scores. If your scores in sequence all fall into this span of numbers, this indicates a very healthy emotional intelligence.

(See your actual score interpretations beginning on page 75.)

INTERPRETING THE THREE MOST COMMON EMOTIONAL INTELLIGENCE SCORE PATTERNS

The profile of the emotionally intelligent individual is distinguished by an ongoing natural balance of emotion and reason. And as you have learned, emotional intelligence is a fluid, dynamic capacity that reflects your sustained ability to integrate your computerbrain's rational capacities with your cavebrain's critically important emotional input. These are the core components that indicate your level of emotional intelligence. The results from the assessments you have just completed will give you a very good idea of how your current abilities compare to the ideal emotional intelligence profile. Consider the following three most common emotional intelligence score patterns:

When Your Score Pattern Indicates Low Cavebrain, Low Computerbrain, and Low Internalization

This pattern is very rare. It generally indicates that you are having difficulty recognizing any of your abilities and feelings and that you are afraid of taking risks and assuming responsibilities. You are almost certainly underrating yourself, which naturally leads to low self-esteem. Repeat the assessment sections again and allow yourself to let the assessment reveal more of yourself to yourself. You will be glad you did.

When Your Score Pattern Indicates High Cavebrain, High Computerbrain, and Low Internalization

This is a very common emotional intelligence pattern distinguished by one central observation: you are reactive. A high computerbrain score shows you that you can be quite rational. You externalize your reactive tendencies and inflict your reactions of self-preservation directly on others, more than on yourself.

Your primal emotion has free rein and you have no effective or consistent way to manage it. Although you are quite rational, you are also quite reactive, and there is no way for the computerbrain to assist because you have never learned how to make the connection between cavebrain and computerbrain.

Inevitably you suffer because of this inability to align your emotions with your reasoning. You continue to act out your emotions, and without being able to manage them, you become even more frustrated because your unrestrained ability to express any opinion seems to be getting you nowhere in life.

When Your Score Pattern Indicates High Cavebrain, High Computerbrain, and High Internalization

This is the profile of the unwitting self-saboteur. As smart as you are and as passionate as you are, you are disappointing yourself in life because you haven't been able to integrate your strong ability to think clearly when you are experiencing intense feeling.

You are second-guessing yourself. You are constantly frustrated and this tends to make your behaviour erratic and self-defeating. When your primal feelings of self-preservation and self-betterment are strong, you suppress any urges to verbalize your feelings or express them outwardly in any way. At these emotional times you use your strong computerbrain capacity not to solve your problems but to initiate your repertoire of self-defeating reactions.

You think about your frustrations a lot, but you don't use that thinking capacity when you really need to, which is when your cavebrain is busy generating such strong feelings inside you. You overanalyze things and, in effect, come up with no concrete decisions or conclusions. You have the inherent emotional and rational tools to turn your life around and the Emotional Management System will facilitate the proper use of these tools. It takes a little study but you are the type of person who doesn't mind putting out the effort when the results it generates are so satisfying. This is the route to the success you deserve.

INTERPRETING YOUR SPECIFIC SCORE RANGES

Before reading your specific score interpretations, please make sure you have added your scores carefully. A mistake in addition will reflect an inaccurate self-assessment.

If, as you review the following interpretations, your score totals fall on the cusp between one score range and another, read both interpretations.

Interpreting Your Cavebrain Score

When Your Cavebrain Score Is Between 0–46

This score falls into the acceptable range. At the lower end of this score range there is very little cavebrain intrusion and, therefore, little impact on how you handle most situations. At the higher end of this scoring range there is a certain amount of cavebrain activity.

Generally you are understanding and obliging, that is, until you feel that people have either overstepped the mark, or there is an issue that is important to you. From time to time you may find yourself feeling a certain amount of impatience, and you can be intolerant of some situations. Provided you have recorded an accompanying low internalization score on the test, there will be times when you choose to express this feeling. At this level, however, there are no indications that this contributes in any significant way to your mishandling of situations.

You tend to avoid situations of potential conflict, and the higher your accompanying computer brain score, the more likely you will justify nonassertive behaviour. This is not altogether a bad thing. This mild amount of cavebrain dominance can provide a ready source of energy and is useful as a self-motivator.

When Your Cavebrain Score Is Between 47–60

At this score range, your cavebrain is definitely active.

Generally you have very clear-cut ideas about how you like things done, but you also have very clear-cut ideas about how you like to be treated. When you feel that you have been mistreated or taken advantage of, your level of cavebrain intensity makes it difficult for you to align your emotional and rational strengths. This level of difficulty increases when combined with a low computerbrain score. This is less so, however, at the lower end of the cavebrain scale.

At the higher end of the cavebrain score, you can become quite reactionary, and you tend to see things in a one-sided manner. In such cases you act impulsively and are reluctant to accommodate an alternate viewpoint. At this stage, discretion is not one of your stronger points. It is difficult for you to learn from these mistakes because your defensive posture stops you from thinking carefully about the issues and considering positive alternative action.

When this score is accompanied by an elevated internalization score or a low self-esteem score, you often choose to express your feelings indirectly or to suppress them altogether in the hopes that the situation will handle itself. Emotional management will help you deal with these emotions and improve your communication skills. Consequently, you will be less frustrated, not as sensitive, and better equipped to handle situations.

When Your Cavebrain Score Is Between 61–74

At this score range, you are experiencing significant cavebrain intrusion.

You are reactive, defensive, and prone to taking things personally. It doesn't take much to elicit an angry reaction from you. When this happens, you lack the capacity to integrate computerbrain input in order to manage these emotions. You are highly energetic, generally quick-thinking, and prone to making quick, firm decisions. Once you have made up your mind, you will not easily entertain an alternative viewpoint.

You do not like criticism and object strongly to being told what to do. This cavebrain intrusion reveals itself in the overall intensity of your character and may well cause problems in your interpersonal relationships.

If this score is accompanied with a low computerbrain score, there is the increased danger of experiencing physical ailments such as headaches. If this score is combined with a high internalization score, it is likely that you suppress your emotions. Your interactions, therefore, tend to be problematic.

When Your Cavebrain Score Is Above 75

At this score range, your cavebrain domination easily intrudes on your actions.

You have a tendency to be aggressive and you can be more than a little intimidating at times. At this level of cavebrain activity it is unlikely that you use much of a computerbrain approach.

If accompanied by a low internalization score, there is little to restrict you and you easily become embroiled in situations. Your response frequently exceeds the demands of the situation. You tend to have preconceived and fixed ideas about many things. You can display a disproportionately intolerant attitude towards people, events, and situations. You are often suspicious of individuals and their motives and this defensive approach makes it difficult for you to accept people at face value.

The lower your accompanying self-esteem score, the more easily your cavebrain will dominate. Even when your intentions are good, your quick temper can often undermine your approach and the outcome you seek. At the higher end of this score range, there are indications that control often eludes you. Possessed of a rigid black-or-white approach, you are volatile, combative, and negative in your outlook. You hold grudges and are intolerant.

Trapped in a cycle of reaction and the consequences of that cycle, you may often conclude that the end results increase the justification for your initial reactions. It is possible that your cavebrain reactions have also pushed you to the position where you are unable to exert post-rational control over your experiences.

If your accompanying internalization score is high, you tend to suppress any outward expression of frustration and anger. At this level, a note of caution is required: this score is likely highly detrimental to you and others around you. In addition to the strategies proposed in this book, you may require help to resolve some of your issues. It may be wise for you to seek counselling and to learn anger management techniques. This combination should prove to be beneficial.

Interpreting Your Computerbrain Score

When Your Computerbrain Score Is Between 47–60

At this score range, it is likely that events in your life have contributed to a lack of computerbrain integration. This causes you to mismanage many situations and it has become extremely difficult for you to balance your emotions with the appropriate level of strategic analysis.

You tend to see things in a one-sided manner, and you are at risk of responding resentfully or defiantly to many issues. You are easily frustrated. You are pessimistic and frequently make decisions that are unwise, especially at the lower range of the computerbrain score.

You tend to be naive about many areas of life. You are extremely sensitive to what you perceive to be criticism, and resent others when they attempt to offer advice. You are at risk of interacting with people whom you view as like-minded and therefore nonthreatening. This illogical bias may place you in the position of being taken advantage of rather than gaining the support you require.

If your accompanying internalization score is high, you will find it difficult to harmonize your interactions, and you seek solace by withdrawing from many situations. This means you may miss important opportunities to resolve problems.

Ultimately you must accept your situation as temporary. By developing your computerbrain approach to issues, you can view your strengths and weaknesses in a balanced way. Once you reach this goal, you can take steps to correct your perceived weaknesses, attain a comfort level, and become self-reliant.

When Your Computerbrain Score Is Between 61–74

At this score range, you have the ability to integrate your computerbrain input over a fairly broad range of situations, but this ability is not sustained at a sufficient level within specific areas of difficulty.

You tend to be sensitive, and with your desire to do well and succeed, you can be self-critical. As a result, you frequently put unnecessary pressure on yourself. However, your objectivity tends to return when you familiarize yourself sufficiently with new or challenging procedures and situations.

When this score is accompanied by an elevated cavebrain and/or internalization score, you risk experiencing a heightened fear of failure and rejection, which colours your approach to a situation. Once these fears intrude, you find it difficult to halt their momentum. They result in your easily compromising logical approaches to your concerns. You then keep yourself from achieving a sufficiently rational approach that would help you to find a reasonable and swift solution.

You could quite easily find that you endure situations for much longer periods than necessary, which results in your feeling confined and stuck in a rut. Unresolved career- or job-related issues will put more pressure on your computerbrain abilities.

You have the desire for change, and the procedures and approaches offered in this book will guide you to finding appropriate self-support. With a clear and systematic approach, plain and simple solutions will quickly emerge.

When Your Computerbrain Score Is Between 75–82

At this score range, you generally function well and approach most situations logically and objectively.

You rationalize and process information well. You have the ability to be concise and thorough. You focus well on objectives, and once you have decided on a course of action you usually proceed in an orderly fashion with a clear-cut plan for attaining your goal.

You have the capacity to cope well with the peaks and valleys that occur along the way, although you may occasionally get bogged down with minor details. With an accompanying high cavebrain intrusion, you have the potential to be highly driven. This combination can result in you making demands not only on yourself but equally on others, which creates conflict from time to time.

At the lower end of this score range, you have a pronounced Achilles' heel: you are prone to more emotional reactions, especially to issues that have an impact on you personally. This will disrupt your focus and result in an unnecessary expenditure of time and effort. Consequently, unresolved issues become more complex than they need to be.

At the higher end of this score range, you are swayed by facts rather than emotion and you apply a rational and logical approach to solving problems.

When Your Computerbrain Score Is Above 82

With scores at this level, your computerbrain does not generally integrate well with your cavebrain. Whereas your analytical approach is highly efficient in objective problem solving (e.g., mathematical or scientific challenges), it rarely functions effectively as an approach to affective problem solving, that is, resolving troublesome personal issues.

Being at this high range of computerbrain ability doesn't necessarily indicate high emotional intelligence. Your analytical skills, while suited to your particular field of work or interest, is accustomed to dealing with finite, quantifiable, and tangible components. Emotional issues, tenuous and intangible, do not fit your problem-solving models. Emotional issues require a less rigid or formal approach. Therefore, you risk becoming endlessly entangled in the complexity of emotional issues. Because you consider yourself capable of resolving issues and have a strong desire to be self-reliant in all areas, your struggle with emotional situations can be a source of compounded frustration.

At the higher end of this score range—and especially when you feel vulnerable, disappointed, or anxious, and early resolution has eluded you—you become overanalytical. This exaggerated approach generates more options than solutions, which creates more potential problems for you. This is called computerbrain entrapment: you are entrapped in a position of non-action and procrastination.

This response is further aggravated if it is accompanied with a high cavebrain or internalization score, and it is even more pronounced if it is accompanied by a low self-esteem score. Any combination of these attributes will result in your experiencing a heightened form of risk aversion, which you justify with a sabotaged form of logical reasoning that supports your inaction.

Getting back on track is comparatively easy because you possess the tools to help you learn quickly. Emotional management will help you balance your computerbrain with your cavebrain.

Interpreting Your Internalization Score

When Your Internalization Score Is Between 0–46

If you have scored in this range and there is an accompanying absence of high or excessive cavebrain activity, this level of internalization indicates that you have a balanced approach to most people and issues. You interact well socially, and you openly express your desires.

When Your Internalization Score Is Between 47–60

At the lower end of this score range, you display a cautious and reserved approach to certain people and issues. In this range, however, the tendency is not negative. Rather, it indicates your desire for privacy and for time to reflect. When this score is accompanied by a high computerbrain score, it reinforces your analytical abilities rather than merely reflecting your desire to withdraw.

If this score is in the mid-range, it reflects a more inhibited nature: you avoid an outward expression of emotions, relying instead on thinking about them.

At the higher end of this score range, your difficulties are mounting. Your sensitivities are more evident and they easily intrude, preventing you from openly proclaiming your opinion even when you are well within your rights to express it. This reticence is exaggerated even further when you are faced with potentially confrontational situations; in these instances, your instinct is to withdraw rather than confront. At this level you tend to allow issues to fester for longer periods than necessary. This wait-and-see approach creates a climate of procrastination, which is partly responsible for your feeling an elevated sense of frustration and discomfort.

When Your Internalization Score Is Between 61–74

If you have scored in this range, you are sensitive and can be highly reserved, although the two traits do not share a cause-and-effect relationship. Consequently, some people at this level demonstrate a mild-mannered approach to events and people.

Your approach to personal issues is definitely compromised by your sensitivities. Once you have adopted a pessimistic approach to an issue, your propensity to hesitate makes it difficult for you to express your desires or opinions openly. You often engage in covert tactics to achieve your objectives in an attempt to reduce your discomfort.

You tend to be self-critical and averse to drawing attention to yourself. You avoid confrontational issues as you find the prospect of such interactions unpleasant. Even when you are clearly in the right in certain issues, your self-effacing approach prevents you from openly expressing your feelings.

You are inclined to mull over issues for much longer than necessary. This wait-and-see approach creates a climate of procrastination.

At the high end of this score range, the potential for procrastination increases significantly. You have a highly withdrawn side. You are reticent about confronting situations, and you dwell on issues for longer than is prudent, which increases your frustration. As a result, the emotional stresses build to the point where, with the absence of an outlet such as cavebrain activity, there are increased risks to your health.

When Your Internalization Score Is Above 74

If you have scored in this range, you are at quite an unpleasant place in your life.

At this level of internalization, your interactions are severely compromised and marked by significant emotional distress. You tend to see your problems in a disproportionately negative light and you are easily overwhelmed. You remain on the outside of situations rather than involve yourself in them.

You are inclined to procrastinate heavily in your attempt to avoid issues that make you uncomfortable. You are at a complete loss about how to take responsibility for your well-being and you easily forfeit control over your issues. At this level you feel trapped inside.

When there is an accompanying absence of high cavebrain activity, your high internalization capacity makes you reluctant to engage in almost everything in your life. Apart from the obvious social, financial, and emotional stresses this reticence can cause, it also constitutes a potential risk to your health as stress and frustration increase.

At this level a note of caution is required: this score is highly detrimental to your well-being. You may require counselling so that you can learn how to resolve the issues that are causing you such distress. This will certainly prove to be beneficial.

Interpreting Your Self-Esteem Score

Your self-esteem score reflects how well you are able to integrate your cavebrain and computerbrain into a naturally and harmoniously functioning system. It is the starting point from which to reexamine your individual cavebrain, computerbrain, and internalization scores.

When Your Self-Esteem Score Is Between 0–28

If you have scored in this range, you have an exceptionally difficult time dealing with situations and people. You often exhibit very negative tendencies and are unable to see the potential for another point of view or perspective. You are frequently caught up in your own suffering and may continually see yourself as a victim. Due to this perception, you often become a victim of others' stronger personalities. You display little self-respect.

You may be exceptionally angry, although you usually take refuge in significant levels of withdrawal from interacting and taking responsibility. You have recognized the need for change but have no way of visualizing the path that would lead to it. You need to be motivated into making the decision to take responsibility for yourself. Emotional management will help you begin to resolve issues.

When Your Self-Esteem Score Is Between 29–49

At this score range, you are aware that the discomforts in your life are detrimental to you. You realize the need for change and you are aware of your self-esteem problem, but you need confirmation that change is indeed possible. You have a history of making sincere attempts to change which have resulted in limited success or even failure.

At the lower end of this score range, you find yourself identifying the details of the problems you face more than the details of potential solutions. Consequently, you may decide that changing the status quo is beyond your capacity.

At the higher end of this score range, your desire to make positive changes is increased, but your generally pessimistic outlook on life tempts you to abandon your efforts. Once you do abandon your efforts, failure and discontent increase the pressure on your self-esteem. This creates a negative perception cycle, a condition which compounds your discomforts and generates more trouble in your life.

At this overall score range, taking calculated emotionally managed risks will produce positive changes. Emotional management is an essential component for increasing your self-esteem.

When Your Self-Esteem Score Is Between 50–60

Scores in this range usually reflect a tendency to place a great deal of pressure on yourself.

You second-guess yourself to the point of self-sabotage. You are a complex, sensitive individual who has trouble trusting your perceptions. The cause of your discontent is usually clear to you, but at this level of self-esteem you are indecisive about how to resolve your difficulties. Your lack of confidence prolongs situations for far longer than necessary and increases the pressure you place on yourself.

The lower your score in this range, the more you are apt to hesitate, and therefore easily compromise your position. At the higher end of this score range, although your outlook is more optimistic, an increase in intensity and turmoil will increase the pressure on your self-esteem. This cycle will ultimately undermine your self-confidence and prevent you from living a balanced, fulfilling life.

When Your Self-Esteem Score Is Between 61–69

At the lower to mid-level of this score range, there are indications of a significant past issue or issues that have remained unresolved. Although this is probably true of everyone at some point in their lives, at this score range your self-esteem is suffering significantly as a result. This increases pressure on your confidence, causes you to second-guess your instincts and generally hold back from taking initiatives. You notice that you occasionally suffer from inexplicable flawed reasoning, which extends into and negatively affects similar but often unrelated issues.

At the higher end of this score range, you exhibit reasonably well-rounded self-esteem and you function well on several levels. When things do not go as planned, you tend to accept limits in your life prematurely. In your quest not to lose momentum or any advantage, you frequently expend more effort than necessary. This results in your often working harder in your life rather than smarter.

When Your Self-Esteem Score Is Between 70–75

At the lower end of this score range, you exhibit reasonably well-rounded self-esteem. Within any skill set that you are confident and familiar with, you function well, although you tend to see the negative aspects of what you are doing rather than the positive aspects. At the high end of this score range, you are relatively self-reliant and enjoy a balanced disposition. You display a normal and fairly healthy approach to the challenges you face daily.

When Your Self-Esteem Score Is Between 76–84

At this score range, you exhibit strong traits of self-esteem. You have a well-balanced self-perception. You are a self-believer and you look to yourself to find solutions to difficulties. You easily take responsibility for your actions, and when things don't go as planned it does not take you very long to rebound.

When your total scores in all areas of this test are within the ideal ranges outlined on page 66, you recognize the healthy challenges in your problems rather than seeing their downside. You therefore implement innovative solutions with energy and focus. You are generally self-assured and maintain a confident outlook about your life and personality.

When Your Self-Esteem Score Is 85 or Higher

A high self-esteem score, which is unsupported by a high computerbrain score and which is further compromised by a high internalization score, is likely more a projection of your desire to succeed and get ahead than any genuine confident and healthy self-esteem. If you have scored in this range, you are likely projecting your desire rather than your actual level.

Even if you have accurately achieved this score range and you have also achieved other scores in the test that are close to the ideal range as outlined on page 66, this level of self-esteem is more complicated than it might seem. Your approach to issues is usually all-or-nothing or black-or-white.

A score in this high range has shifted you out of balance and at this level can produce a very aggressive, defensive, and highly opinionated personality profile. This will not necessarily prove effective in solving problems or improve your approach to people and situations. With your inherent perfectionist inclination, you risk forcing your opinions onto others, and you are reluctant to entertain alternate viewpoints to your own. You are also intimidating and rigid, and display a conspicuous reluctance to admit your own faults. You maintain an emotional intelligence pattern that is out of balance and cause for concern.

(Note: It is rare to score in this range for this test. Please check that your answers reflect your genuine feelings about yourself and that you have accurately totalled your score.)

WHERE DO YOU GO FROM HERE?

Now you have some idea of where your emotional intelligence pattern fits on the emotional intelligence scale. So where do you go from here? Let me assure you of something: very few people in today's high-pressure society actually fit into the ideal emotional intelligence pattern outlined on pages 65–66. We all have a weak link in one area or another. The great news is that you can use the insights and strategies presented in this book to transform those weak links into strong foundations.

Given the tremendous power of the cavebrain, you might legitimately be asking yourself: Do people actually have the capacity to find rational solutions in the midst of an emotional barrage? Do they work with a different set of cognitive tools than mine? Do they succeed in life where I haven't yet? The truth is that yes, you can integrate the computerbrain with the cavebrain's responses. You have all the tools within you to successfully make the integration, and you can achieve anything you set out to.

Once you have transformed weak links into strong foundations, you will have the ability and the willingness to recognize the importance of failure and tragedy. You will notice how astoundingly inaccurate perceptions are when the cavebrain is dominant, and you will see how these factors operate together to damage self-esteem. But most of all, you will begin to recognize that there is a way of turning your life around by taming the cavebrain.

You must not allow yourself to be tyrannized by the cavebrain. It will rule you when you don't understand how it works or how to integrate it with your computerbrain. Part I has given you a deeper insight into yourself. You are now ready to examine the full impact of cavebrain domination, as well as the key initial steps that will help you integrate your computerbrain's input with your cavebrain's powerful emotions.

In Part II, you will explore the cavebrain-dominated life. You will begin to see how a lack of emotional intelligence affects you and those around you. You will see how your self-esteem struggles to support you in such situations. And as you begin to see your own distinct way to free yourself from relying on your cavebrain foundation, you will discover a natural Position of Independence that lets you live life with inner strength, self-respect, clear direction, and purpose.

Journal Entry

Life is an infinity of divisions
Divided into infinity,
And paradise a sugar-coated lemon
The fools that fill the divisions
Are an irregular lot—knowing not
That they are not what they aspire to be
And if I knew the reason
For my being—and my foolish words,
My title would be Sage

PART II

TAMING THE CAVEBRAIN

THE EMERGENCE OF EMOTIONAL INTELLIGENCE

The emotional management test you completed in Part I illustrates that the interpersonal challenges we face have more to do with our cavebrain reactions than most of us would care to admit. Having taken the test, you are now in the position to view your emotional terrain more objectively. As you examine your scores, you may be asking such questions as: How do my cavebrain reactions affect how I cope with the stresses in my life? Wouldn't it be better for us all if we could get rid of the cavebrain somehow? Doesn't it cause more trouble than it's worth? How do I start to bring my powerful rational capacities into alignment with my powerful emotions?

I asked myself these questions many years ago. I struggled with the power of my own intense emotions and my reactions to them. I was using my cavebrain so intensely that nearly every emotional reaction I felt related to self-survival. Is that the way your cavebrain works for you? Probably.

The insight I had into the purpose of this cavebrain capacity is simple: immediate emotions are there to protect. Once you realize this, you can engage the computerbrain to find rational solutions to your problems.

The cavebrain's intentions are good. We need it, not only to protect us from danger but to motivate the computerbrain to find rational solutions to personal problems. However, the cavebrain is not intended to find long-term solutions. It is like the mini spare tire in the trunk of your car. It is not intended to be used on an ongoing basis; it is a temporary solution designed to help you cope with the immediacy of a predicament and give you the opportunity to initiate a long-term solution.

When you rely on cavebrain reactions for an extended period, you deny yourself the energy you need to devote to finding a long-term solution to your problem. As time passes and you begin to calm down, you are able to deal with the problem more rationally. This is the first indication that the cavebrain and computerbrain are integrating in order to help you solve your problem effectively.

UNDERSTAND YOUR CAVEBRAIN IN A NEW WAY

When you observe it from the standpoint of human evolution, cavebrain dominance is not the common attribute of today's fittest and most balanced individuals. The equation is really quite simple: people who rely on their cavebrain reactions are, on the whole, unhappy and unfulfilled; people who allow their cavebrain to cooperate with their computerbrain are, on the whole, happy and fulfilled.

We are ready to step beyond the dominance of the cavebrain. We have arrived at the moment of transition from cavebrain dominance to cavebrain-computerbrain cooperation. Most important, you are reaching the point of your own personal evolution. Your life is about to change, it is about to improve and open into the dynamic and rewarding life you have always hoped for. And it can be achieved naturally and easily. What is the key factor that will drive this evolutionary push? Popular terminology refers to it as emotional intelligence. And you are learning the system that I refer to as emotional management—the ability to integrate the functioning of our primal reactions and emotions with our advanced capacity of thought and reason.

There is no reason to accept any limitations in life. We have the capacity to integrate thought and emotion which, once understood, can help us move beyond the cavebrain's instinctive and often restrictive way of reacting to create a far more productive, exciting, and enjoyable way of living. Emotional management is remarkably simple because the key to it is found precisely where the problem is found: in the brain's capacity to react or problem-solve.

Your thoughts and reactions can be managed so that you can achieve your goals. Emotional management will show you how to minimize excessive reliance on the cavebrain and maximize the integration of the cavebrain with the computerbrain so that you can always find powerful and effective solutions to the issues that confront you.

Emotional management will not eliminate your emotional struggles. Rather, it will give you the tools to embrace your struggles and engage your natural capacities to arrive at effective solutions. It will speed up the process of distancing yourself from your initial cavebrain reactions and integrating the essential input of your computerbrain.

You do not have to suffer forever. If it usually takes you weeks of suffering before you find balance, you now have the opportunity to reduce the period to a few days. If it normally takes you days to recover from an emotional blow, using emotional management, it can now take hours.

The Emotional Management System is a powerful tool. Let us now celebrate the lows in our lives that spur us on to achieve the highest of highs.

Journal Entry

I wish you to understand me
For I wish to understand you
Accept me and I can accept you
Let me love and respect you
And I can only hope
I know what I am
As I continue to
Grow into life

THE JOY OF HITTING BOTTOM

Everyone's definition of hitting bottom is unique. But we all know what it feels like. It feels like the end of the world. We try as hard as we can to find a way up, but nothing seems to work. We feel hopelessness, despair, frustration, and devastation. For those who use their inherent tools, however, out of struggles come solutions.

We invest a tremendous amount of energy and thought into emotionally charged moments. Ironically, it is this deep amygdala–cavebrain emotion that prompts your neocortex-computerbrain to search everywhere for a solution. The frustration that you feel at times of crisis does not arise from your inability to perceive your situation; you certainly know the fix you are in. The real frustration arises from the fact that you don't know how to take the energy you are feeling and apply it systematically to find a solution.

NFL QUARTERBACK FALLS FROM HERO TO ZERO

When we think about hitting bottom, we frequently think of celebrities whose falls always capture our attention and appear to be so much more dramatic than our own.

Art Schlichter's experience is a good example of such a fall. Schlichter was a former American high school and college football star and local hero in the state of Ohio. He became a top first-round pick in the National Football League draft, and signed a highly publicized contract with the

Baltimore Colts of the American Football Conference. Ostensibly, Schlichter was living the fairy-tale life of the quintessential American athlete, but by the time he reached the NFL he was suffering from a crippling addiction to gambling that would turn that fairy tale into a nightmare.

Schlichter began gambling in college in an attempt to relieve stress. The young prodigy was repeatedly chosen for quarterback positions over more experienced players who openly resented that they were being passed over for the fabulously talented upstart. By the time Schlichter turned pro in 1982 he had gambled away his entire signing fee from the Colts. By 1983 he was losing more money in one week than his entire annual salary. And by 1984 he was banned from playing in the NFL.

"Even football people who suspected I had a problem kept quiet, because it would ruin my career," he told *People* magazine. "But they knew something was wrong. I was a horrible player. I couldn't concentrate. It was as if I'd lost all my skills. Emotionally, I was shot."

Schlichter managed to keep earning money for his habit by playing quarterback for teams in smaller professional leagues across North America, until he was injured and lost his job. In 1989, the year he got married, he was caught writing a bad cheque and received a suspended sentence. Apparently chastened, he entered a rehabilitation centre to try to kick his gambling addiction. He dropped in and out of the program, actually gambling at a frantic pace at the same time as he was going through rehab.

In a recent interview, Schlichter discussed this tragic period in his life. "I wasn't ready for (my therapy) to work. I hadn't hit rock bottom. I actually felt I would die if I gave up gambling. It took jail to bring me out of my fantasy world."

Schlichter reached rock bottom in 1994 when he was incarcerated for bank fraud, having tried to cash cheques from his sister-in-law's closed bank account. This was the depth that Schlichter needed to reach before complete awareness of his dilemma convinced him to make a change in his life. He is now out of jail and trying to put his life back in order.

Schlichter's is the kind of riches-to-rags story that highlights what can happen to us when we are unable to manage our stressful emotions effectively. Studies of compulsive gambling show that the problem usually affects bright, charismatic men between 21 and 55 years of age. Ironically, further assessment reveals that typical gamblers such as Schlichter suffer from loneliness and very low self-esteem—afflictions all of us can recognize, and which many of us struggle to reverse.

I HIT BOTTOM IN 1970

Unlike celebrities like Art Schlichter, for most of us, hitting bottom is a very private experience that can open the door to transformation.

In 1970 I was a very different person from the one I am today. I was demanding, fearful, rigid, and arrogant. I was overly aggressive and dominated by emotion. I was surviving. I was up, I was down. Up, down. Up, down. There was no equilibrium. One day I would be in seventh heaven where things could not be better, and then at the slightest frustration, I would plunge into deep depression or give way to rage. Everyone who knew me described me as the quintessential angry young man.

My anger was my energy and protection. It was the driving force that propelled me towards achieving what I wanted and protected me from what I didn't want. All this I accepted as normal. Moreover, I could justify my actions by blaming the past.

My childhood was not the easiest or most pleasant. I was the first, and only, child, born into a second marriage, welcomed by my mother alone. My authoritarian father was incapable of showing affection and warmth. He hugged me once during his life. Consequently, I often felt rejected.

My emotionally abused mother, who found herself battling with two stepchildren as well as me, tried to control my natural youthful exuberance through a paradoxical mixture of unrestrained love and dire threats to send me to the local orphanage. Added to this was my two older half-brothers' resentment of me. Their mother had died tragically, and whatever the reality, they perceived me as privileged and spoiled, even if that privilege was confined to the simple position of having a biological mother. For all I knew, this was what growing up was supposed to be like.

There are no schools where parents can learn how to be parents. There are no second chances. What you get is what you've got, and I got an unhappy childhood. I had a father who never showed me love and a mother whose inner turmoil was amply transformed into my deepening inner pain. Not surprisingly, sympathy seeking became my all-consuming pastime in an attempt to ease my discontent and gain affection. My efforts were futile, and I became even lonelier and sadder and angrier, day by day.

As a young adult, I used anger as a source of energy which I poured into my work. I was determined to make up for my childhood. I told myself that life needed to be like soaking in a hot bath while eating a bowl of cherries—warm, secure, relaxing, innocently sweet and delicious. I was fortunate that I had decided to channel my energy towards success, because I could have just as easily let go the line altogether. So, as long as my ups were longer than my downs, I was okay.

But who was in control of my life? Was I actually in control or not? Could I wake up in the morning and decide how the day was going to be, or where I was going? I didn't think so. I didn't believe anyone could. I never allowed anyone to penetrate my invisible walls. They formed a reliable and effective defence, or so I thought.

My childhood was a series of emotional disasters and triumphs of survival. I was an emotional, insecure wreck. As I grew up and began to focus on creating a stable, secure environment, I was able to apply myself to genuinely rewarding and legitimate enterprises. Given the wild drama of my childhood, it amazed me that people believed that I was in control. They accepted my mood swings as part of my personality. I was always quick to laugh. I dressed well. I looked the part of the successful man. People excused my behaviour, saying: "He's the creative type." "He's sensitive." "He's just Paul."

In fact, I had never been lower emotionally. I visited a number of therapists in my quest for understanding and direction, but all I received were numerous prescriptions for antidepressants and rigid stopwatch endings to my sessions. I sank deeper and deeper into depression. My world began to crumble. I realized that I was no longer in charge of my life. I had allowed circumstances to control me. I hardly slept at night and suffered acute anxiety attacks when I did fall asleep.

THE TURNING POINT

One night I woke up bathed in sweat. I couldn't breathe and shooting pains darted across my chest. Was I experiencing my first heart attack? In a panic I drove to the hospital. Before I knew what was happening, I was whisked past the patients in the waiting area and into an emergency trauma unit. A team of physicians descended upon me, wiring me to an electrocardiograph, taking my blood pressure, and checking my heartbeat. Their obvious concern made me panic even more.

After about five minutes, the doctor in charge told me to relax. He told me that I was not having a heart attack; I was experiencing a massive spasm in my pectoral muscles. He warned me that such intense spasms are often the result of extreme inner stress. Whatever the source of my tension, he said, I had to find a way to turn myself around, because at the rate I was going, I might actually suffer a heart attack. I was so wound up, so highly strung that my body was reaching its limit to handle the stress. His prognosis terrified me.

At that moment I realized that I could not continue living the way I had been living, with my angry reactive personality and my laundry list of justifications to support my self-destructive attitude. I had to change.

RECORDING THE EFFECTS OF MY MISALIGNED EMOTIONS

My strong emotions showed me what I wanted and what I didn't want, but my rational thinking had to be just as strong so I could achieve what I wanted, and distance myself from what I didn't want. I had to learn emotional management. I began to write philosophical observations in a journal and list my perceptions about my emotional reactions. These were the seeds of what became the Emotional Management System. They were the motivators of my early higher rational thought. (I have included some of these journal entries at the conclusion of several chapters of this book.)

Rereading my philosophical observations, I began to discern the cavebrain processes that shift emotions out of alignment with reason and cause such havoc. Through this expressive exercise, I was secretly hoping to discover that I was, indeed, highly rational, and that by identifying some basic behavioural patterns I could redirect my life.

As I studied the journal entries, I began to notice surprising correlations, and few of them were flattering. I wasn't really behaving like a rational human being. I was living like a caveman, a *cavebrain* man.

I wondered why it was so hard for me to behave rationally when I was experiencing intense emotions. And how had I ended up with such a lousy self-image? While I did not realize it at the time, I had begun to identify the capacity of the amygdala cavebrain to knock our emotions out of alignment with our rational faculties. I was defining the "system" of chaos that prevents us from using the innate skills we use to get through the days when we are not bombarded by emotional stress.

Self-examination can be torturous yet extremely rewarding. I would lie awake for hours thinking. Then it came to me: I had many outlooks to consider—social, religious, political—but no system that helped me manage my emotions and my life. I needed to find a systematic way of dealing with my strong emotions. I had to find out why primal emotions so relentlessly controlled my life. More than that, I wanted to survive and thrive, lower my stress level and fulfill my potential. It would take me years to develop the core components of the Emotional Management System.

THREE CHEERS FOR FAILURE

Hitting bottom in 1970 was one of the most important experiences of my life. For many, however, hitting bottom reveals itself less dramatically, through errors and failures. Just as I value the nowhere-but-up viewpoint, I consider failure to be an equally constructive experience. Failure often marks the path that leads to success. Sometimes failure is how your view of yourself and your world manifests itself so that you can see on the outside what you are feeling and holding on to on the inside.

Mistakes give you the chance to move forward. Each mistake teaches you something. Each mistake leads you to another step. With each mistake you learn. In the words of Winston Churchill: "We must learn from misfortune the means of future strength." Consider this concept for a moment: Nothing actually stays the same for very long. We are all in perpetual motion, constantly moving. In this motion we achieve something, whether it is something greater or something dubious.

When you stand still because you are afraid to do anything for fear of making things worse, you become stagnant. You are, in effect, moving further into your failure. Making a mistake is part of the learning process. It's part of a positive action. The biggest mistake you can make in life is not to make any mistakes.

Think about it. Which events do you recall most about your life: the successes or the failures? If you're like most people, you recall the failures initially. And you recall them because you were not in control. But failures nearly always promote higher emotional intelligence. Why? Because beyond the initial reaction (pain), you are forced to consider new approaches that will help you avoid the situation in the future. You are forced to stop and think about yourself.

I once looked back on my life, at every lousy, rotten thing that ever happened to me. At first I thought, how could any of those things have benefitted me? I discovered that each step forced me to change my direction. By changing my position, I realized that I had moved forward. At first the disappointments knocked me backwards. Since I didn't like where I was, the only alternative was to find a way to move forward, even if it was only to avoid the pain.

So, what does it mean to hit bottom and fail? It means you are at that glorious evolutionary stage in your life when your perceptions of yourself and all that surrounds you are coming into question. It hurts like hell, but hitting bottom can be the most fruitful time in your life if you approach it correctly. This is your opportunity to grow and evolve as never before. This is your opportunity to see yourself in a new way by learning how to see your life experience in a new way.

Journal Entry

Insecurity
obviates reason
Security
Treasured only
By those
who have suffered
Taken away by those
who have not

8

THE POWER OF PERCEPTION

Your personal evolutionary shift begins by understanding the building blocks that create your identity, especially those building blocks that represent obstacles to your growth.

PERCEPTION—THE ROOT OF THE PROBLEM

Traditional learning systems have been a source of enormous frustration for me. I knew that if I wanted to make my personal evolution work, I would have to understand everything in minute detail. To learn something, I have to understand it at its most basic level. I combine this basic understanding into a step-by-step practical application. I challenge it, rearrange it in my mind so that it makes sense. I have learned that for something to work effectively and efficiently I have to visualize the first step and how each step leads to the next. Many of my students who also have trouble with conventional learning have discovered that this method works for them, as well.

To develop a new and powerful method of self-transformation, I began with a study of the dynamics of perception. I needed to understand what perception was and what role it played in shaping my decisions. The more I examined the power of perception, the more I marvelled at how easily perception can distort our view on life and how these distortions quickly become absolute truths. What an amazing revelation that was. Surprisingly, this very adult analysis led me to consider a fascinating moment in my childhood.

Fooling Circus Elephants

I grew up in Hillbrow, South Africa. One of my most vivid childhood memories is of the circus parade that came to my city. Hillbrow is a large metropolitan city, where the closest thing to a wild kingdom are the pigeons that harass you as you walk down the street.

One morning I woke up to the sounds of music, the trumpeting of elephants, roaring of lions and tigers, and myriad other exotic noises. The circus had come to town.

I raced down to the field where tents were being set up and wandered around, wishing that the lion tamer would ask me to help him or that an acrobat would show me some tricks.

I loved the smell of the circus and the feel of straw beneath my feet. It was such a contrast to the concrete jungle I lived in. I looked into the cages and marvelled at the ferocity and magnificence of the creatures they contained, never once thinking about the stress these once-free animals experience behind bars.

I was intensely drawn to the elephants. These were the giants I could actually walk up to and touch. There was poetry in the moments I watched as an elephant I had thrown some peanuts to gently picked them up with its trunk and ate them. I always approached these gentle giants cautiously and stood there for a long time, mesmerized by their sheer size, before I could pluck up the courage to stroke their tough, prickly skin. But I did. It was magical.

Perhaps my love of elephants was spurred by the fact that they seemed to be so accessible. They were not caged like the other animals. They were, however, restrained around one ankle with a metal cuff attached to a thin chain that was held by a small peg driven into the ground. I concluded that these majestic creatures were passive and easily controlled.

Fooling Wild Elephants

When I was an adult I directed a documentary on the wildlife in the Oko-vango Swamps in Botswana. This area is often described as one of God's playgrounds. The Okovango is a region of contrasts. Desolate salt flats and heat-baked former seabeds extend mile upon mile to the horizon. On these white solid salt cakes nothing grows, and the only noise you hear is the sound of your tires moving along the barren paths. At the same time, the Okovango forms an oasis in the middle of a desert and hosts myriad wildlife from flamingos and vultures, to crocodiles, lions, cheetahs, zebras, wildebeest, and elephants. As you glide along in a dugout, you look down through the paradoxically crystal-clear water of the swamp and observe the snow-white trails gouged by hippos as they run along the swamp floor.

One day, as our convoy reached the far edge of a clearing, I spied a herd of elephants grazing on the branches of tall acacia trees. I had never seen so many elephants gathered together in one spot. It was a spellbinding scene.

I noticed how incredibly protective the elephants were of their young. The matriarchs would watch over the babies and nudge them gently away from any perceived danger. At one point the herd banded together to pull a baby elephant out of a deep muddy ditch. At no time did the herd panic. Rather, it appeared to make a plan, and one by one hauled and pushed the baby out of the mud. It was a seemingly endless task yet they persevered tirelessly. At last, when the young elephant was safe, the rescuers rubbed their trunks reassuringly along its side to express their delight at its return.

Our guide cautiously led us steadily closer to the elephants, motioning us to be very quiet. We stopped behind some trees and gazed at the herd. After a while, I noticed the guide repeatedly picking up fistfuls of sand, then slowly emptying them onto the ground. When I asked him what he was doing, he said, "I'm checking the direction of the wind." He explained that elephants have very poor eyesight, which is why we were able to venture so close to them. However, he pointed out, they have an excellent sense of smell, and if the wind shifted, our scent would quickly reach them. The bulls of the herd would then almost certainly confront us.

I was confused. "Why would the elephants want to charge us?" I asked the guide. "We won't harm them. In any case we are well protected behind these trees. If they do catch our scent, we'll pack up and go." I said these last words confidently because I had always thought of elephants as very slow animals.

If the bulls perceive a threat, the guide told me, they will charge immediately. The trees offered no protection because elephants can push them over as easily as we pull weeds from the ground. He also informed me that elephants can run at a speed of approximately 25 kilometres an hour.

My mind raced through a series of scenarios featuring immense elephant tusks goring us to death, then I thought back to the elephants at the circus. Had I missed something? On the one hand, here I was, watching elephants ripping mature branches off trees because they had depleted the supply of smaller trees. On the other hand, I recalled circus elephants restrained by a small wooden peg approximately one foot long, tiny compared to the large branches that offered little obstacle to the elephants I was observing in the wild. I was confused. I asked the guide the obvious question: How could a circus elephant be restrained by a small wooden peg, yet be capable of uprooting large trees and ripping them to shreds, branch by branch?

He explained that when the circus elephant is very young, animal trainers drive a thick stake into the ground and attach a chain to its leg. The baby elephant isn't strong enough to dislodge it, even though it tries over and over. At some point, it simply gives up. Even though the elephant is the strongest animal on earth, it learns that it cannot free itself, and so as time passes it gives up trying. The size of the chain is changed to accommodate the elephant's growth, but the restraining stake remains unchallenged. What also remains unchallenged is the elephant's perception that it cannot free itself.

Perceptions and misperceptions, I realized, are tremendously powerful. As long as a perception remains unchallenged, it constitutes whatever you perceive to be the truth. It amazes me what we hold as truths despite evidence to the contrary. Our perceptions dictate that something is "true." It seems we need to observe the perceptions and misperceptions outside ourselves to begin to appreciate the limits of our own.

Fooling Wild Game

You could argue that the circus elephant is conditioned because the only reality it knew was captivity, and you could argue that in the wilds perceptions do not carry the same influence. But this is not so. Consider another wildlife story.

After we completed the Okovango documentary, our film crew was invited to follow a group of game wardens as they began Operation Springbok. Their objective was to move a herd of about 300 springbok, a southern African gazelle.

Moving wild game is difficult because, obviously, before they can be transported they must be captured. This feat is accomplished in an astounding manner. A keyhole-shaped structure with eight-foot-high walls is erected across the plains. The springbok are then channelled towards the wall by helicopters and noisy mopeds. The springbok run, spring, and leap away from the cacophony, but are driven inexorably to the ever-narrowing enclosure. Then suddenly they are in the enclosure. Confronted by the walls, they stop. As the choking dust settles, an eerie silence descends, and quietly, almost serenely, the springbok are funnelled one by one into the waiting trucks. The capture works with incredible precision.

The most interesting part of the story is this: the walls that constrain the wild animals are constructed of paper. Even the weakest springbok could challenge the walls and leap through. But they do not. This method is used for all game. The great wildebeest—the African buffalo—are stronger than the springbok, but they too are stopped by the paper walls because they believe that the walls are impenetrable. The truth is, the animals are entrapped by their own perception. The walls maintain their strength because the animals perceive that the walls are impenetrable and they do not challenge those perceptions.

An uncontested perception generates its own reality: perception equals fact. The circus elephant perceives that it cannot move the stake so it does not even try. The wild game perceive that the herding walls are impenetrable and so they stop within them. These are graphic examples of the power of perceptions and misperceptions.

You must learn to challenge your perceptions. How many paper walls have you erected in your life? How easily do you accept what appears to be fact? How many uncontested perceptions have prevented you from achieving your goals, whether it is to resolve a problem, create new opportunities, or advance your career? Many people underestimate the power of perception. Far too many don't acknowledge that perception can ever equal fact.

Fooling My Own Eyes

You could argue that humans are more intelligent than animals and could never be so easily subdued into accepting such simplistic reasoning. Consider the following story:

A couple of years ago I broke my glasses. Not only can I not see without glasses, but because I also develop terrible headaches without them, I always have a spare pair on hand. I have also developed the habit of putting things where I know I can find them, then promptly forgetting where that place is. This time I couldn't find my spare pair. Frustrated, I tore around the house frantically looking for any old pair that could tide me over.

I put on an old pair that I had worn a few years earlier. The weaker prescription made seeing difficult. I took off the glasses and cleaned them, and accepted that even though they were far from perfect, they were better than nothing. I struggled miserably through the day. I knew that I was wearing the wrong prescription, and the more I thought about it, the more irritable I became.

When I went to the optician, I explained that I was having difficulty seeing clearly with this outdated prescription. She took the old glasses, measured their prescription strength, cleaned them, and handed them back to me, gently smiling. "These are the same prescription as your existing pair," she told me, "so you shouldn't have difficulty seeing."

I looked at her sceptically. She couldn't possibly be right. And yet when I put the glasses back on, I could see perfectly. The blurriness disappeared as quickly as it had appeared. A new fact emerged along with the new perception: there was never anything wrong with the glasses, but because I was convinced that I was wearing a weaker prescription, I perceived that I could not see correctly. Perception and perception alone created its own truth, which misled me with convenient ease.

Fooling Ourselves

Think about how your perceptions create your reality and influence your decisions. How many uncontested perceptions create impenetrable walls because we do not test our primal amygdala-cavebrain perceptions? How powerfully do your perceptions entrap you in situations you believe you are helpless to resolve?

The degree to which perceptions control the way you function is extraordinary. Perceptions either work for you or against you. They either prevent you from trying to change when you believe that you can't or they motivate you to find solutions when you believe that you can.

How many people do you know who are convinced they can't achieve their dreams or who can't seem to elude their torments? How many people do you know who have stopped trying? How many dreams have you given up because of your perceptions? And how many goals have you achieved because you either believed you could achieve them or didn't devote any thought to why you couldn't.

Perceptions are not to be instantly relied upon. Learn how to challenge them, because only by questioning them can you start to confront the paper walls that entrap you, and set yourself free. You can only do this, however, with a disciplined approach that you can rely on. Whatever your perceptions and however strong your conditioning, emotional management will help you to challenge your perceptions to make sound decisions that support instead of sabotage you. The Emotional Management System will enable you to perform at peak levels of emotional intelligence.

PERCEPTIONS WILL PLAY OUT THEIR ROLES

Susan is in the medical profession. She is in her mid-thirties, attractive, and successful, but she has never been able to sustain a lasting relationship. I discovered that when she was a child her father repeatedly told her that she would never be good enough for anyone to want to marry. It seemed that her father's prediction was fulfilling itself. When I asked Susan what she thought the problem was, she said, "It's just that the men I meet are so much better than me. They're more sophisticated, more intelligent. I don't feel that it's fair for a man to end up with someone who can't meet his expectations."

What intrigued me about Susan's litany of rationalizations was that at no time did she think there was anything askew in her perceptions. How was it possible that every man Susan was attracted to was better than she was? Remember, Susan is an attractive, successful person. Yet each time she was interested in a man, her feelings of unworthiness intruded and she quickly ended the relationship before it had a chance to grow. Even when a man paid her compliments, it made no difference; she dismissed them with comments like, "Oh don't be ridiculous!" She believed that she didn't deserve a healthy relationship because she perceived that she didn't amount to much. She believed that she had very little to offer. Just being herself wasn't good enough. Her perceptions ensured that her life experiences conformed to her self-defeating beliefs.

Would it be fair to say that there is very little difference between Susan's acceptance of facts and the circus elephant's? Would it be fair to compare the springboks' physical entrapment within paper walls to Susan's emotional entrapment by her acceptance of perceived facts? It would be fair indeed because there is no difference. Perceived facts are accepted facts, even when they are not true.

Susan accepted her lot in life with glib phrases like, "This is me." She tried yoga and weekend getaways in the hope that these activities would repair what was wrong. These approaches, however, didn't work to her advantage. She needed to move from the inside out, carefully and systematically. She needed—and ultimately applied—the precepts of the Emotional Management System.

Today Susan's changed perceptions have armed her with a set of positive "facts." Ten years after her personal journey began, she is a happily married woman with a beautiful family. Once she was able to deal with her feelings of unworthiness and to manage them from a more rational position, she discovered that she could commit herself to a relationship. This is not to say that nagging doubts and feelings of unworthiness never haunted her again, but when they did she was able to manage them effectively.

THE TYRANNY OF NEGATIVE INPUT

Just as the circus elephant's self-perceptions kept it a prisoner, so too does the cavebrain conspire to re-create the conditions that present self-misperceptions as absolute fact.

We react to negative stimuli far more readily than positive stimuli. We always feel greater urgency when dealing with negative input, and we always feel less in control. A negative stimulus causes a negative emotion like fear, anxiety, or discomfort. We cannot ignore this emotional input. It demands our immediate and undivided attention. It is important. It is survival.

The cavebrain is programmed to process threatening stimuli in order to protect you. It is committed to the survival motive. Negative stimuli prompt instant responses because to your cavebrain they represent danger. That's why you respond immediately with a core range of protective emotions: anger, fear, rage. Your cavebrain creates the necessary reaction to these "facts," often supporting the most negative conclusions about your worth and potential. You do not apply the same urgency to positive stimuli because you process them differently. The absence of threat automatically suppresses the need for a cavebrain reaction.

We are tyrannized by negative stimuli. Take smoking, for example. Cigarette packages prominently display warnings about the dangers of smoking. These dire messages are supported by media campaigns that show in graphic detail the most ghastly side effects of this habit. So why do these warnings not stop people from smoking? Smokers dismiss them because the cavebrain perceives no *immediate* danger to their tobacco consumption. Many young people who take up the habit are caught up in the idea that it's "cool" to smoke. Yet many smokers who experience a serious smoking-related illness quit immediately. It takes a personal negative stimuli to make them quit.

What are the personal negative stimuli that are prompting you to change? Are you overwhelmed by the events in your life? Is it a problem in your relationship with a loved one? Is it a serious problem at work? The same paradigm applies: the cavebrain kicks in because it perceives mortal danger and the survival motive becomes operative. Negative emotion generates an immediate reaction. The immediacy of these emotions convinces you to act in your best interest, and instantly you react.

You trust your lifesaving cavebrain implicitly, and well you should. You don't think through lifesaving reactions. If an oncoming car drifts onto your side of the road, you don't pause to consider why or how it is happening; you react. That is the way your cavebrain is programmed. But, as discussed earlier, operating exclusively from your cavebrain is not beneficial, especially when you are experiencing sustained periods of stress.

THE PECULIAR COMFORT OF DISCOMFORT

When you are unhappy, confused, or lonely it is easy to kick into and remain in cavebrain mode and adopt what appears to be your safest position. The line of least resistance makes it easy to foster and legitimize negative emotions. It is easy to mistake cavebrain reactions to pain for the computerbrain's role of taking personal responsibility. Often, denial is a powerful persuader. Many people who look back on a personal crisis once they have emerged from it see how negatively single-minded they were. They are shocked that they didn't realize how many options were available to them at the time. When you are in these highly charged situations and your cavebrain dominates your thought process, you will not be able to recognize alternatives.

Ask yourself if you would prefer being happy to being sad. The answer is a no-brainer. Of course you would rather be happy. Do you want to be in a position where you feel that you are in control, or would you rather be in a position where you feel you can't cope and your life is out of control? Of course you prefer to be in control. It is unnatural to want to be an emotional wreck. So why can't you just switch from sad to happy, unmanageable to manageable, emotional to rational? Without a system of emotional management accomplishing this feat is almost impossible. Your cavebrain is programmed to react to what it perceives as danger and not stop reacting until it perceives that the danger has passed. It is only when you look back at your own situation, or at someone else's, from a logical perspective that you can begin to see how perceptions create facts which you follow blindly.

I was having lunch with a client, Daniel, when I noticed how nervous he was becoming. As we ate, he visibly changed. His face turned a grey-white, and his physical demeanour began to resemble that of a frightened animal. During our conversation, he seemed to drift off as if his thoughts were somewhere else. I asked him what was wrong.

"I don't know," he said. "I don't have a good feeling."

I asked him, "About what?"

"I have a meeting with my boss at two."

"So what?" I said.

"I've been away for three weeks," he told me, "and I don't have a clue why he wants to see me."

Clearly, Daniel was seeing the prospect of this meeting in an entirely negative light, and it was distressing him. He was obviously expecting a negative outcome. "So, what are you basing your total apprehension on?" I asked him.

He replied, "I don't know. It's just a feeling. I just can't trust this guy."

There were no facts to base his "feelings" on, yet he was becoming more agitated by the minute. I marvelled at his pure cavebrain reaction to his perceived situation. After questioning him for any further justification, and finding none, I reassured him that absolutely nothing out of the ordinary was going to take place at the meeting. My reassurances did nothing to alleviate his cavebrain's reign of emotional terror.

I asked him to contact me after the meeting to let me know the outcome. The meeting was, in his words, a "nonevent." Released from his cavebrain's strong hold, he returned to his bright, good-humoured, cheerful self. Moreover, he was unable to even recognize his previous apprehension.

I am not surprised at how easily we respond to negative input, even perceived negative input. Think about how often you have been told "no" in your life. You've probably heard the word far more often than the word "yes." As a result, consider how you automatically respond when you've been hit with a negative. Think of your emotional reaction. Think about how immediately emotional your reaction is.

Once the cavebrain takes over, even positive intentions go awry. I recently saw a parent slap her child because the youngster did not get run down by a truck. Her actions don't seem to make sense. Visualize the parent watching in horror as her child dashes across a busy street without looking. In a near panic the mother showed her intense relief that no harm came to her child by physically punishing him. This is the nature of our primal emotions. The mother was in full cavebrain survival mode, wanting to lash out at the source of danger to her child's life. She couldn't attack the truck, so she lashed out at the closest thing to the danger: the target, her own child.

On the surface, the mother's actions make very little sense. After all, the child didn't notice the truck in the first place, so darting into traffic wasn't a volitional action on the child's part. The parent's punishment then was actually directed at the child's ignorance, and if the child didn't have the awareness to notice the truck, all the child can connect the punishment with is the act of walking with his mother. The mother's computerbrain didn't engage her cavebrain, and as a result, both the mother and child have learned nothing and the parent has come no further to helping the child learn to avoid danger. The mother has simply produced another form of physical injury that the child will try to avoid.

Another example of cavebrain response comes to mind: Raquel had been suffering from a deep depression for more than a year and had been taking Prozac for eight months. Her depression was caused by both career-related and personal problems.

Raquel was a teacher. At work she experienced stress arising from constant criticisms of her teaching methods by her supervisor. She tried to change her approach, but that did not stem the criticism. Whatever she did, the supervisor berated her. Raquel decided that this individual was hoping she would cave in under the pressure and leave, which would pave the way for a personal friend of the supervisor's to replace Raquel.

As for her personal life, Raquel's boyfriend of four years had left her. To make matters worse, within five weeks of their breakup, he had moved in with another woman. When Raquel heard about this, she took a two-week leave of absence, locked herself in her apartment, and cried for a fortnight. Not only did she regard herself as a failure professionally, she also believed that she was a failure in her relationships.

Raquel's reaction to her professional and personal problems was excessive, you conclude. There were other, more constructive options open to her: she could have reported the supervisor; and she could have realized that many couples split up. Moreover, you may insist, she should have been able to get over the crisis without resorting to medication.

It's easy for us to make rational judgements on events; we are not emotionally involved, and therefore not working from cavebrain mode. From our computerbrain point of view, it is easy to process information systematically, consider options, and choose an appropriate course of action. Raquel's problems at work had a long history, and the split with her boyfriend was the proverbial last straw. Her cavebrain reaction instantly responded. Her immediate perception generated an instant perceived reality upon which she became fixated and the "facts" remained uncontested.

AN EXERCISE IN CAVEBRAIN-COMPUTERBRAIN INTEGRATION

Think of a situation that troubles you—a situation heightened by emotions. Do you seem to "know" all its negative aspects instantly? Has your mind frozen with indecision because all decisions seem to lead to the same negative conclusion? Are there seemingly no alternatives? And if there are, do they all promise to make matters worse?

Now ask yourself this question: Have I tested the validity of the perceptions that form the foundation for my conclusions?

Now consider: Do you truly know what the facts are, or is it possible that there is more to your situation than your cavebrain is allowing you to examine?

If you have answered these questions quickly because you already know the "facts," you are still stuck in cavebrain mode.

Ask yourself: Is it possible that I have remained so engrossed in the facts as I perceive them that even as I read this I am convinced that the facts are the facts? They may not be. Perhaps you have manacled yourself to facts that bear a questionable validity. Perhaps they are not facts at all. Has your cavebrain quickly assured you that you are absolutely correct or has your computerbrain begun to question the validity of your perceived reality? It is time to question your facts now.

Try this simple exercise. Write down your problem on a piece of paper. Record your purpose and list your options. Divide the paper with a line down the middle. Put the pros of the issue on the left and the cons on the right. Partialize the problem, that is, break it down into sections. Put all the "impossible" conclusions aside and pick the easiest part of the problem to tackle.

Sample Exercise

Problem: I have not spoken up for myself when I thought I should have. Now I feel angry, resentful, and frustrated.

Purpose: To focus on the pros and cons of the problem and dismantle the cons.

List options: 1. Speak out for myself

2. Not speak out and hope the situation improves on its own

[In this example, we have chosen option 1—to speak out.]

PROS of Speaking Out	**CONS of Speaking Out**
1. I will no longer feel put upon.	1. I could make matters worse.
2. I will have more self-respect.	2. My co-worker could respond more aggressively.
3. I will be taken more seriously.	3. I will be perceived as pushy and rude, or as a person who overreacts.
4. I won't feel so frustrated.	4. I will compromise my position and become even more stressed.
5. I won't end up doing things I don't want to do.	5. I will jeopardize my position and status.
6. Overall, I will experience less stress.	

Partializing: I dismantle the cons by ensuring that I prepare myself to eradicate or handle each one correctly.

[We'll use one con to show you how this is done.]

Con 1 I could make matters worse.

Partialize: • If I leave the situation as it is, does it get better, stay the same, or does it potentially get worse?

• What steps do I take to ensure that matters don't become worse? (i.e., take ownership of the issue—don't blame)

• identify the exact issue (i.e., Is it the way I was treated? What exactly did I object to?)

• How do I approach the person?

[The more you can break it down and reveal its components, the easier it will be for you to tackle the issue and create a plan of action which you can then follow. You learn more from your mistakes than from anything else.]

What alternatives have you come up with? Is it possible that there are other alternatives? By completing this exercise you have introduced a computerbrain approach to your situation. You have begun to use an emotional management technique. You may not arrive at a solution instantly. That may take hours or even weeks. But you have begun to exercise the computerbrain. This is the only way you will find truly effective solutions to emotional management problems.

The above exercise is not intended to be a complete technique for integrating cavebrain and computerbrain thinking. What it does is illustrate that you can use an intellectual technique to address an emotional issue. Consider the exercise and look at what happened the moment you began to work through your problem. Look at how you began to approach your problem differently once you'd separated out its component parts. Look at how alternative solutions, no matter how improbable they may have appeared, became tenable. This is the exciting impact of cavebrain-computerbrain interaction.

Your cavebrain is survival-driven but it does not always precipitate action that is in your best interest. What you need to achieve is a personal outlook that allows you to act in your own best interest. I call this personal outlook the Position of Independence (PI), because when you learn to act from this position you discover that you can quickly manage your emotions, and that you need never again be an emotional victim. In Part III, you will learn a complete method for achieving cavebrain and computerbrain integration to reach your PI.

Let's get back to our distressed teacher for a moment. I encouraged Raquel to approach her situation in the manner described above. She recognized her need for a Position of Independence. Once she learned to partialize her problem, she learned how to manage her emotions, analyze her position, and wean herself from Prozac. She was then able to reorganize her perception of work. She learned that her supervisor wasn't trying to get her fired, but that her teaching style indeed needed improvement. She also accepted that while she was very hurt when her boyfriend left the relationship, there was nothing wrong with her. It was the relationship that was wrong.

Raquel was able to readjust her perceptions only once she'd moved forward. Until that point, Raquel's life spiraled downward. One of the most interesting facets of Raquel's story is how distorted her perceptions were. She perceived that the supervisor wanted to get rid of her. When her colleagues argued against this belief, Raquel's misperceptions reinforced her "fact" that now everyone was against her.

Self-misperception not only reinforces your own limited view of yourself, it can also send you into a debilitating downward spin that feeds upon itself and multiplies into a series of debilitating conditions that sabotage you. Once these invisible walls are in place, perceptions create their own reality. You accept anything you believe you can control and reject anything you believe you cannot control. Indeed, reality is primarily what you perceive reality to be.

NEGATIVE PERCEPTIONS NEGATE ALL SUCCESS

The force of self-misperception filters through and affects our life experiences. Consider Simon's story.

Simon and I grew up together. He had an older brother, Patrick, who excelled at everything. He was the captain of the rugby team and class president. If Patrick entered a competition, he invariably won. If he auditioned for a play, he came away with the lead. In a debate, he always won hands down. He also had a marvellous sense of humour. Everyone loved and admired Patrick.

Simon was very talented in his own right. He was quick with numbers, a strong defence on the rugby team, and very creative. Unfortunately, he never once stopped to consider his strengths. Instead, he constantly compared himself to his brother to whom, Simon believed, he could never measure up. Poor Simon. He always felt that his brother was the favoured son. Furious, Simon would pound his fists on the wall and complain, "It's so unfair! I can never do anything right! It's always Patrick this, Patrick that! Don't Mom and Dad realize they have two sons?" He believed that his parents loved Patrick more than they loved him and this self-perception reinforced his belief that his brother was luckier, better educated, more intelligent, and therefore would always be successful, while he, who was not as lucky, would never be a success.

Today Patrick is a successful professional. Simon, on the other hand, has never made a success of anything, which is tragic because he really has so much talent. He has started a number of ventures which all showed a lot of promise but which invariably failed. The pattern is always the same. He begins with an abundance of enthusiasm and energy, then at the first sign of trouble, he convinces himself that his project will never work. He lines up the usual excuses: the recession is killing him, or he is promoting the wrong product, or there is no demand for his idea. The venture fails. Even as a child, Simon displayed that same pattern. Every time he started something, he would give up and fail.

Simon's story is a classic example of the self-perception circle. Simon's negative self-perceptions negate all his potential. His perception that he will never be as good as his brother overrides every chance he has of success. The truth as he sees it remains unchallenged. All that is really holding him back is his own self-misperception.

Simon's story is not unique. People fail to measure up to their potential because their perceptions dictate that they cannot succeed. What holds people back, however, is not their lack of skills but their inability to test their true potential. It is only by challenging your perceptions that you can soar to the heights you seek.

Unfortunately, Simon did not learn the Emotional Management System and he is still succeeding at failing. Once you learn how to challenge your perceptions through emotional management, you gain amazing insights into your true potential.

IF PERCEPTION ISN'T REALITY, WHAT IS REALITY?

When you are emotionally charged, reality is primarily what you perceive reality to be. That is not an earth-shattering revelation. You have certainly experienced that the more you are hit with negative stimuli, without a set of positive stimuli to balance them, the lower and lower your self-esteem falls. Look again at your emotional intelligence test results (Chapter 6). These results indicate precisely where your strengths lie and, more essential for personal growth, where your difficulties lie.

There is a way to begin to sharpen your perception so that you don't become a slave to your perceived reality. There is a way to examine your tremendously powerful self-perceptions. There is a way to undo the damage that these beliefs may have caused. There is a way to become self-reliant, independent, and strong. You are about to bring that method into your life.

Journal Entry

To trust oneself
is divine
To falter creates the chance
to seek further
the source of one's control

9

REPAIRING THE DAMAGE TO YOUR SELF-ESTEEM

Cavebrain reactions can send you into an emotional tailspin that keeps you out of control until you can apply a rational perspective to an uncomfortable situation.

It sounds simple, doesn't it? The trouble is, if you have tumbled into a tailspin, the original problem you were facing is often combined with a damaged self-perception. If left unattended too long, this can further damage your self-esteem. The more you face a bombardment of negative stimuli in the absence of positive stimuli, the more your dependence on those negative perceptions weakens your self-esteem.

You are about to learn how to permanently release yourself from dependence on negative perceptions. You are about to learn the keys to genuine personal independence. This is your opportunity to re-establish your self-esteem by re-engineering your self-perception.

REVIEWING YOUR LEVEL OF SELF-ESTEEM

Your self-esteem is the foundation for everything you do, from how you react to situations to how you handle them. Self-esteem and communication are linked. Consider the following equation: healthy self-esteem provides comfort. When you are comfortable, you can communicate. When you communicate, you increase your comfort level. This process of communication continually builds and maintains your self-esteem. On the other hand, damaged self-esteem restricts everything you do, from your perceptions to how you communicate.

The key to effective self-management is understanding how your level of self-esteem affects everything you do. It is the key to understanding why you may feel unhappy or unworthy.

Based on your level of self-esteem, you will project a positive or negative image. How do you think people describe you when they meet you? What are your best qualities? Would they describe you as warm and friendly? Outgoing? Tolerant? Perceptive and sensitive? What about those qualities that people don't like when they meet you? Would they describe you as aggressive and intolerant?

How would you describe yourself? When I ask people with healthy self-esteem to describe themselves, their self-assessments are usually accurate. However, when I ask people with low self-esteem to describe their best qualities, they describe the traits they wish they had rather than the ones they actually possess.

Having completed the emotional intelligence test in Chapter 5, you have a profile of your current level of self-esteem and how it relates to your level of emotional intelligence. Review your scores in Chapter 6.

UNDERSTANDING THE SELF-PERCEPTION CIRCLE

Learning how to gain control over your self-perceptions is crucial to success in life. How often do you think others have judged you either negatively or positively based on how you perceive yourself? What impact has this had on your life, your career, your success?

Your self-image is a constructed belief pattern—a biased belief built upon opinions that begin with you and that are ultimately fed back to you. In other words, the way you see yourself strongly influences the way other people see you. They pick up the messages you send them about how you see yourself. They consider and accept those perceptions. Having accepted this opinion, they behave toward you accordingly. You, in turn, pick up the messages people seem to be sending you about yourself and react to it. It becomes a vicious circle. Unknown to you, you actually initiate this circle. People's reactions to you don't independently confirm your feelings about yourself; they simply reflect your own.

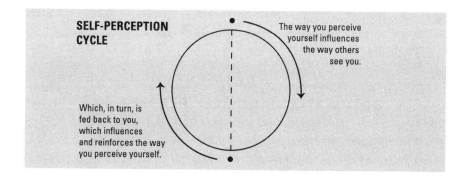

THE FEEDBACK LOOP

When I first met Carolyne it was obvious that she was shy. Everything about her—the way she spoke, what she said, what she didn't say, the way she walked, her lack of eye contact—contributed to my perception of my new student. When I interacted with her, I altered my body language regularly to accommodate her shyness. I softened my voice when addressing her, and treated her in a gentler, almost cautious way, much the way one would handle a fragile vase.

I was interested to see the different ways people in the class treated her. Some approached her with indifference, some with impatience. Some were kind to her, others were rude. The response she received from other people formed the feedback loop that served to reinforce Carolyne's perceptions of herself: we noted her shy manner and treated her accordingly; this treatment, whether gentle or insensitive, reinforced her perception of herself.

Carolyne, on the other hand, was very aware of how people treated her husband, Larry, who attended the same class. Larry owns a landscaping business. He is outgoing and confident. Throughout the sessions, Larry was often asked for his opinion during discussions. He was obviously a decision maker. He led conversations while others listened. He commanded respect easily.

Carolyne longed for the kind of recognition and attention Larry received. However, she allowed her self-perceptions to reinforce her belief that she didn't have what it took to get it and that even if she did, she didn't deserve it.

You begin to see the dynamics of the feedback loop. Carolyne is shy; Larry is confident. People treat Carolyne as a shy person. People treat

Larry as a confident man. Carolyne improved a great deal once she learned to recognize how the self-perception circle operates and how, in fact, she initiated the cycle.

NOT CHALLENGING SELF-PERCEPTIONS

Most of us don't challenge our perceptions. When your perception tells you a situation is hopeless, you accept self-imposed limitations as facts and give up trying to solve your problem. You latch on to obstacles rather than objectives. The longer this sorry situation persists, the greater the damage to your self-image. And in the end, your self-esteem suffers.

In emotional situations people tend to focus on the negative. In difficult situations your emotions are more active than usual; the cavebrain is active. As various negative perceptions are introduced, they dominate your focus. You spend a disproportionate amount of time and energy focusing on the negative and avoiding what you don't want to happen as opposed to embracing what you do want to happen.

When your emotions run high, your cavebrain steals the energy you need to think clearly and logically. It is a universal phenomenon that affects even the most rational people. My sister-in-law is a prime example. She is a perpetual optimist and a self-appointed cheerleader for anyone in trouble. She is self-assured, confident, and well-meaning. She eagerly offers her advice to anyone experiencing emotional difficulty; that is, unless the person experiencing the emotional difficulty is herself. Then she reacts like all of us. She has difficulty challenging her perceptions. She reacts. She is incapable of the kind of energetic affirmation she offers to others. Suddenly, the "facts" of her condition are, in her opinion, unchallengeable. They are real, fixed, and immobilizing.

IDENTIFYING BARRIERS TO HEALTHY SELF-ESTEEM

When you are a victim, you become trapped by your predicament because you are only capable of focusing on the obstacles. The situation is very real for you. You can feel your pain; you can't feel your hope. Emotion prevents you from rationally investigating alternatives.

Your imposed and self-imposed limitations mount as you recite the numerous factors that justify your state: lack of control over other people, lack of experience, feelings of guilt, financial considerations, fear of loss or rejection, fear of failure. When you are confronted by a problem, these factors are entirely real to you.

You convince yourself that you don't know how to approach your situation. The idea of freeing yourself from it is contradicted by your self-perceptions. The "facts" entrap you. And so you undermine your capacity to stand up for yourself or to act in your own best interests.

MY MOTHER—A PRODUCT OF THE SELF-ESTEEM FEEDBACK LOOP

My mother is one of the most talented people I know. She had a terrible childhood. Born before World War II she was raised by a strong-willed Russian mother who had never learned to read or write but had the wisdom of Solomon. Unfortunately that wisdom did not extend to her three children—all girls, all from different fathers.

My mother lived with a stepfather who hated her. My grandmother did nothing to intervene, and told my mother that she would not allow her to jeopardize the marriage. At the tender age of 16 my mother realized that she was no longer welcome in her own home, and she went out to fend for herself.

Fifty-eight years later, my mother is described by everybody she meets as funny, charming, and talented. However, she has wasted much of her extraordinary talent because of her lack of self-esteem. She has sacrificed countless opportunities because she convinced herself that nothing would come of them. She became a model as a teenager but never devoted herself to the career. When she married, she didn't learn to drive because my father told her it was too difficult. She writes brilliantly humorous film and television scripts but never tries to get them produced.

If my mother had fully applied her considerable talents, she probably would have been an extremely wealthy, successful woman. But here again the self-perception cycle loops its way around, reinforcing initial perceptions, and without a spike to drive through the wheel and stop it, nothing changes. You have to want to change in order to learn how to change. If you believe you can change, then you can. After all, perception equals fact. If you believe you can't, that too becomes fact. As Henry Ford said, "Whether you think you can or can't, you're right."

Journal Entry

Truth has many sides,
its credibility determined
by which side you
happen to be on

10

STABILIZING THE SELF-PERCEPTION CIRCLE

Think of your place in the universe. For 1,400 years people believed the 2nd century Greek astronomer, mathematician, and geographer Ptolemy, who theorized that the sun, planets, and stars revolved around the earth. You can't blame him. After all, that's how it looked up in the sky. That's what he perceived as fact. And anyone who looked at the sky could have come up with the same theory. The 16th century Polish astronomer Copernicus questioned Ptolemy's "reality," and used mathematics to prove that the earth, spinning on its axis once daily, revolves annually around the sun. In the end, he proved that the accepted facts were wrong.

What about your facts? Do you believe that your life revolves around and depends upon the whims and dictates of others? Maybe it does at this point. With a new perspective, perhaps you can prove that you have been deceiving yourself. Perhaps the facts you have been believing about yourself, or your current situation, rest on some pretty shaky foundations. Perhaps you are the one who creates your own facts. Perhaps you create your own universe.

Don't trust the facts about your life. Facts can be notorious falsehoods, especially when it comes to accepted negative conclusions about yourself. It takes effort to challenge your perceived facts. But you can do it. A little inspiration can help you get yourself in gear.

REWRITING THE "FACTS" OF LIFE

In 1985, Dr. Thoralf Sundt, chairman of the Department of Neurosurgery at the Mayo Clinic, and one of the world's leading neurosurgeons, was diagnosed with multiple myeloma, an incurable cancer of the blood cells and bones. The experts' prognosis was that Dr. Sundt had six months to live.

This remarkable man decided that he had too much to do and that six months was insufficient time to do it in. Not comfortable with the facts about his life, he chose not to accept them.

Six and a half years later, in September 1991, Dr. Sundt was featured on the television newsmagazine "60 Minutes." Although he was in constant pain at the time and needed special equipment to help him stand, as well as a special brace to protect his ribs from breaking under his own weight when he slept, he worked a full schedule, which included operating each Monday, Wednesday, and Friday. Dr. Sundt chose to live. His challenge was not to defeat cancer, but to live with the disease for as long as he could. He achieved his goal and continued to perform delicate neurosurgery, thus helping hundreds of people to live healthy lives. Dr. Sundt eventually succumbed to the disease, but his remarkable achievements stand as a testament to the power of re-writing the "facts" of life.

Creating Your Own Luck?

I often ask my training groups to reflect on their past achievements. On one occasion, Colin, one of my students, told us how he had immigrated to Canada from the island of St. Vincent in the Caribbean, with no assets, and how in virtually no time he became a successful businessman. I asked him what he thought contributed to his success. He shrugged and said, "I don't know, I guess I was just lucky." Lucky? Imagine if we could all attribute our successes—and failures—to good luck, or bad luck? If we did, what would happen to all of those who aren't lucky? Would they stand a chance?

Digging a little deeper, the group discussed why Colin had succeeded. From the moment he decided to immigrate to Canada, he never stopped to consider the possibility of failure. He never focused on obstacles. He focused only on his objective. It burned ferociously in his mind. He fleetingly considered the difficulties he might encounter, but he didn't dwell on them. He admitted that had he known what the immigration ordeal entailed, he might never have attempted it in the first place. But he was preoccupied with his determination to succeed. His objective was so clear that he did not stop to consider his achievements as accomplishments. They merely became steps in the process, each step bringing him closer to his goal.

RELEASING THE FEAR OF SUCCESS

How many areas in your life remain unchallenged because your self-perceptions remain unchallenged. Would your life change if you could improve your education? Would it change if you changed your career? Can you become the person of your own dreams? Can you improve the relationships in your life?

We all accept limitations about ourselves. These are perceptions. They will never change unless you test them. Only then can you challenge them. Only then can you test their validity. And only then can you begin to make the fundamental changes that will turn your life around. You *can* reinvent yourself.

REINVENTING YOURSELF

When you learn how to challenge your perceptions you will change your approach to life. You will discover that you can be decisive. You will become more independent and do the things that best serve your interests, free from uncontested perceptions and beliefs that have been imposed—or self-imposed—and free from dependency and self-doubt. Ignorance and intolerance survive best when there is an absence of determination and dialogue. Dependency thrives when you forfeit your self-worth.

Consider the following four criteria that lead to significant life change.

Change Criterion 1: The Simple Act of Noticing

Awareness is the prime mover of change. It is unlikely that you will want to attempt change in your life until you become aware of the need to change. This may sound like an oversimplification, but think about it for a moment. The only reason you take in your car for unscheduled repairs is that your awareness has been alerted somehow, perhaps by a disturbing noise in the vehicle somewhere or by an activated warning light on your dashboard. When you start receiving and noticing the warning signals about your life, it is time to investigate and focus on change.

Caroline Knapp, a Boston writer, wrote a book called *Drinking: A Love Story*, a chronicle of her battle with alcoholism. The daughter of a prominent psychiatrist and professor at Boston University, Knapp slid into the drinking disease easily, and early. She lived in a traditional household in which the open display of strong emotions was frowned upon. Instead of expressing emotion, her father soothed his soul with alcohol. Knapp began drinking during her prep school years, and before she knew it, liquor had become, in her words, "the single most important relationship in her life."

After her parents died, Knapp became withdrawn and anorexic. The turning point in her life came one day when she called her sister on the phone after work, only to realize that she had spoken to her sister the night before but was unable to recall the conversation or even that they had spoken. Knapp suddenly became fully aware that she was in trouble. This awareness initiated her gradual recovery and return to a more rewarding and fulfilling life.

Change Criterion 2: Balancing Discomfort and Hope

There must be a balance between discomfort and hope to prompt change. Discomfort generates motivation. On the other hand, comfort frequently generates complacency. When there is an absence of hope, there is an absence of incentive. Returning to the car analogy, the discomfort arises once you become aware that there is a problem with your vehicle. The incentive (or motivator) occurs when there is hope that the car can be repaired. Ultimately you want to achieve a balance between discomfort and hope. There will always be a benefit to you personally.

Mark Lenzi won a gold medal in diving for the United States at the 1992 Olympic Summer Games in Barcelona, Spain. He quickly became one of America's superstars and media heroes and basked in the glow of fame. Unfortunately, the glow faded quickly, and fortune never came for him. He suffered through a severe case of the post-Olympic blues, living off his meagre savings, drinking heavily, overeating, and gaining 30 pounds. He had reached his rock bottom.

Mark's transformation began to occur when he realized that his sport would never generate his fairy-tale dream of fame and fortune. More important, he realized that he loved the sport simply for the joy of it. He had been through his discomfort and now he longed for another opportunity to test himself in the Olympics. Mark returned to serious training to prepare for the 1996 Olympic Games in Atlanta. Even before he tried out for the Olympic team, Lenzi had another hope: to return to Indiana to study meteorology after the Games were over, and to begin the rest of his life. Mark finally found the balance he needed between hope and discomfort.

Change Criterion 3: Focusing on Objectives, Not Obstacles

For positive change to occur, you must be able to focus on objectives, not obstacles. I find it fascinating that nearly all my students focus on precisely what they do not want to happen instead of on what they want to achieve. You must be able to clearly define and understand your objective. In other words, you must know and understand exactly what it is you want. Without a complete focus on your objective, you risk focusing on the obstacles in your path. The more difficult your circumstances, and the lower your self-esteem, the greater the risk of sabotaging your success.

Jacquelyn Mitchard is a columnist for the *Milwaukee Journal-Sentinel*. She is also the head of a large family. Her husband died in the early 1990s. Suddenly she was not only faced with the daunting task of raising her children alone, she was also confronted with the desperate need to earn enough money to keep her family clothed, fed, and sheltered in the home they had always lived in.

Jacquelyn had very definite objectives, one of which was to write a novel. With $86 in her bank account, she began to write *The Deep End of the Ocean*, a riveting story about the disappearance of a child. After receiving only seventy pages of the manuscript, Viking gave her a $500,000 two-book contract. The novel was published to rave reviews. Actress Michelle Pfeiffer optioned the movie rights for $300,000.

Mitchard focused on her objective and hung on to it. She was undaunted by perceived obstacles and inspired by her dream.

What are the obstacles you perceive you face? And, more important, what are your objectives?

Change Criterion 4: Managing Negative and Positive Stimuli

Negative Stimuli

Negative stimuli can lead to positive stimuli. Negativity can force you to find alternatives. The trouble is, we accept the negative more readily than the positive. Why? Because we need to control the out-of-control. Moreover, we are conditioned to accept negative stimuli. As far back as we can remember, negative stimuli have been used as a control mechanism. As children, how often did we hear threatening statements? Far too often for most of us.

Recently I observed a mother struggling with her two-year-old during a packed flight from Toronto to Fort Lauderdale. The child, confused and frightened when she found herself in cramped, unfamiliar surroundings, began crying. She shouted, "I want to get out!" The girl's mother, who in a more private environment would likely have resorted to screaming back at her daughter, did nothing. She offered no reassuring comments and made no attempt to pacify her distressed daughter. She provided nothing but stone-cold silence. Imagine, here is a distraught child who is becoming more hysterical by the minute and she is greeted with a wall of indifference.

Now imagine if the mother said to the child, "If you don't stop crying I'll call the captain, who will remove you from the cabin and put you in with the baggage." Or, "If you don't stop crying, the captain will take you off the plane and mummy will leave you all alone and you'll never see me again."

This sounds impossibly negative, doesn't it? Yet millions of parents attempt to initiate change in the behaviours of their children by offering as an alternative a proposal that is far more negative or threatening than their children's current predicament. This is done in the hope that rhetoric will somehow improve the situation, not for the children but for the parents. This type of negative stimuli has a devastating impact on an individual's self-esteem.

Your self-esteem will support you positively or negatively. The self-perception circle reinforces the input. It is a well-known yet sad fact that adolescents often seek negative reinforcement in the absence of its positive counterpart. Consider youth gangs, for example. New members readily subject themselves to violent and inhumane initiation rituals in order to be accepted by the group. They do this because they need to be accepted, somewhere, by someone.

I am not suggesting that you seek out negative stimuli in order to affect change. I am suggesting that we all crave acceptance or change and we take it any way and anywhere we can.

Positive Stimuli

Positive stimuli invariably triumph over negative stimuli and lead to healthy change. There is a judge in the United States, for example, who sentences young offenders, many of them gang members, not to jail but to dance and acting classes. This may sound absurd, but the results speak for themselves. The positive reinforcement that the young offenders receive during these "sentences" has turned many an ardent criminal into a peaceful and law-abiding member of society.

In an example of the power of the four criteria to effect dynamic change, an American senator who was severely verbally and physically abused as a child and who also witnessed the verbal and physical abuse of his mother, believed his voters would reject him if they knew about his past. He kept his secret for many years. In 1994, during a congressional investigation into spousal and family abuse, he was motivated to speak out on the issue. His change of mind could not have occurred until all four criteria were present: He was aware of the traumatic effects of his abuse (awareness). When he realized that if he didn't speak up he would end up being part of the problem and not part of the solution (balance between discomfort and hope), he was able to distance himself enough from his perceptions to logically define and focus on his objective. The stimulus that triggered the change was the negative stimulus associated with the investigation into abuse.

Divulging his past did not lose the senator votes. If anything, his honesty made him stronger and reinforced his credibility with his constituency. As long as he focused on obstacles such as losing votes, he could not move forward. He could not control his destiny. This is the kind of recurring theme you face when you are hopelessly caught up in your problems. Your focus is always on the obstacles and never on the objectives. Thus, you never move forward.

There is no rule that says that positive stimuli will result in a positive outcome or that negative stimuli will effect a negative outcome. It is very much up to you and your circumstances, and that's the point. Very often negative stimuli are the catalyst for a positive outcome. Positive stimuli can likewise effect a negative outcome. But there is one crucial rule that you follow whether you want to follow it or not: life will control you unless you learn to manage your emotions.

You *can* learn to manage your emotions, and it all begins with learning how to achieve emotional independence.

Journal Entry

Yes. I will love, hate, destroy,
build, rise and fall
For that is my experience
and if I am not broken,
perhaps one day I will
deserve my title "human"
and have a place in society
The only danger then is
all the other learners

11

ESTABLISHING EMOTIONAL
INDEPENDENCE

You are the sum total of your thought processes. The process goes something like this. You get emotional a lot. That's human, of course. You react emotionally and get yourself into hot water. That's human too, but it's only part of being human, and it's where most of us limit our personal growth. You have learned that the cavebrain often dominates your thought processes. And you know that you often feel that you are not in control.

You now know the protagonists of the emotional management drama. Cavebrain (amygdala). Computerbrain (neocortex). Perception. Self-esteem. Each seems to have its own agenda. What is really going on here? Your low self-esteem is often formed through a misperception of the facts. You twist your own perceptions. Your cavebrain takes over the process of self-identity. Because the cavebrain processes input before the computerbrain can get hold of it, it generates an emotional reaction that is, in fact, most often completely unsupported by the computerbrain input that will produce a meaningful and enriching resolution.

YOU'VE LEARNED TO MANAGE, BUT THE WRONG WAY

As you have seen in Parts I and II, it is clear that the cavebrain's motives are predictable and that it performs in a remarkably systematic manner, which at times leaves you and your emotions out of whack. As a result, you suddenly perceive realities that aren't realities, you base decisions on facts that are fiction, and in the process you alienate the very people whom you need on your side. Most of all, though, you begin to damage your self-esteem, your sense of inner independence.

Your emotions have been shifted out of alignment with your reasoning. The skills you normally use when you successfully solve the many problems you confront every day are suddenly undermined by the momentum of your emotions. And when you find yourself in the throes of the confusion, despair, frustration, and anguish generated by your cavebrain, in the absence of an alternative experience, it is the anguish and despair that you will sustain.

Whether you realize it or not, you have learned to manage your emotions systematically. No one ever wrote down the system and you won't find it in any textbook. Your parents, teachers, lovers, friends, and enemies all wanted you to think and behave in a way that pleased them. Step by step you learned a system of thought that defined your pattern of emotional reactions, whether that system suited you or not. You accepted these suggestions and tried them out. Some worked for you and some didn't. As long as this pattern of cavebrain reactions continues unchecked, however, you will not know how to stick a wrench in that process and give the computerbrain a chance to think logically and reflectively.

Wouldn't it be great if you could stick a wrench into the system that throws your emotions out of alignment? And wouldn't it be great if you could then use that wrench to realign your emotions so that you could perform at an optimal level and achieve your most cherished goals? The Emotional Management System is the wrench that realigns your emotions. And it is a tool that you will master, using the fundamental insights you learned in Parts I and II.

You have arrived at a new position in your self-awareness. You have not only learned the basics of how the brain processes emotion, you possess the tools to enable you to question the rules by which you have allowed your cavebrain-computerbrain to function. Now you are in a position to integrate your cavebrain and computerbrain efficiently and rewardingly so that you can put yourself in charge of your emotions and in charge of your entire life. What you need now is a management system that will permit you to interpret all the input you receive then process it in a naturally balanced, systematic way that ensures you identify the facts that really *are* the facts, feeling emotions that are based on actual facts, then responding in a natural way that enriches your life.

IF YOU CAN'T BEAT THE CAVEBRAIN, JOIN IT

This is the whole idea: by joining forces and using your computerbrain to effectively integrate your cavebrain's instant reactions, you can begin to incorporate a way of managing your emotions that actually supports your own best interests and the best interests of those around you.

Behaviourists have long recognized that we are not only creatures of habit, but that we are capable of implementing and adjusting those habits in periods of approximately twenty-seven days of reinforcement. That is, if you want to change your behaviour in a particular area, it will require about twenty-seven days of consistent disciplined behaviour to integrate computerbrain solutions with cavebrain responses. In effect, you are not bypassing or cutting off the natural functioning of the cavebrain. You are not doing anything unnatural. You are simply following a more rewarding set of rules—a system that can help you achieve a Position of Independence.

In Part III you will learn how to support your cavebrain reactions with your computerbrain thinking using the Emotional Management System.

Journal Entry

I hear sweet music
My life expands with the sound
I smell the aroma of a multitude of flowers
And my head becomes dizzy
Yet the tomorrows that are to come
Are capable of disguising these feelings
And nostalgia does not exist then.
Am I capable of striking an equilibrium
Between these two extremes without losing
The beauty of hearing sweet music—
And the smell of sweet flowers?

PART III

THE EMOTIONAL MANAGEMENT SYSTEM

LISTENING OPENED MY EYES

I never would have discovered the transformative power of the Emotional Management System had it not been for my persistent curiosity and Bob Grant, my first employer. Mr. Grant taught me the essence of emotional management by showing me how he used a conscious wedge in his interpersonal relationships. I am convinced that Mr. Grant had no clue he was teaching me anything at all. What he did have was one powerful mind, and I learned through his example.

TAKING STOCK AT RADIO HILLBROW

I was about 14 years old when I got my first part-time job. It was at Radio Hillbrow, Mr. Grant's electronics store in uptown Johannesburg, South Africa, where I grew up. It was a very small store and times were tough, but Mr. Grant agreed to hire me. It was a typical part-time job. I stocked shelves, helped customers find merchandise, and went door to door delivering flyers.

Mr. Grant was a little stern (probably because as a 14-year old I didn't have the world's most diligent work ethic), but he was always fair and very encouraging. When I was 15 he promoted me to store manager, which was really a storeroom manager. The new title made me feel important and successful and worthwhile, which was more than I was ever made to feel in my own home. That sense of importance was something I desperately needed at the time.

Another quality that impressed me about Mr. Grant was his ability to listen. When customers came in with an appliance that needed fixing, he didn't just ask them what didn't work then tell them he'd figure it out. Rather, he let the customer explain the vagaries of the malfunction for as long as they wanted to. It amazed me that he went through the same rigmarole with every customer, when I was certain he had gone over virtually the same problem with some other customer the same day or a week ago or months ago.

One afternoon, after a customer discussed in painstaking detail a common malady with the wringing rollers on a tub washing machine, I asked my boss why he spent so much time listening to the customer when he probably already knew what the problem was. "I don't listen for what people need," he said. "I listen for what they want. That's how you build relationships in business and in life."

Somehow I knew that his message was important, and so it stuck in my head. It didn't begin to form the essence of what would become the Emotional Management System until a year later when I experienced one of the most traumatic events of my life.

I was 16 and earning 45 rands a month (a very modest sum, equivalent to the income earned delivering a daily newspaper in a large neighbourhood). I was living at home in a basically dysfunctional environment. I was headed in every direction and at the same time I was headed in no direction.

I came home from work one day at about 6:00 p.m., and my mother, who was wrestling with her own demons at the time, decided that I had to have a bath immediately and go to bed early. Naturally, I was outraged. I was 16 going on 50 and wondering why on earth I should suddenly be ordered around like a 5-year-old. We got into a terrible argument and she said, "If you don't like the rules and you don't like it here, get the hell out." (Her language was actually quite a bit more colourful.) I replied, "Can I really go?" She said, "Yes. If you refuse to do as you're told, get out. Leave. Leave right now." I suspect that my decision to take her up on her offer probably both frightened and infuriated her.

As I was getting dressed to go she stormed up to me and probably more in an attempt to frighten me than anything else, she said, "No, no, no, no. If you want to leave, you leave now!" I was wearing my trousers, no shirt and no socks, so I grabbed a jacket and shoes. I was ejected from my home like an unwelcome guest being thrown out on the street. As I opened the front door, my father, who never missed an opportunity to impose his will, said, "Give me your front-door key." In other words, "You leave now, you leave for good."

I stood motionless with my shoes in my hand and looked him in the eye for a moment, then haltingly dug out my key and handed it to him. The door slammed hard behind me. I ran barefoot down the stairs and into the world with just a jacket on my back, tears streaming down my cheeks, nowhere to go and without a penny in my pocket. I shudder at the memory.

I had to try to find someplace to sleep. I could not go to a friend's. It was too temporary a solution. So I arrived at a residential hotel in the hopes of renting a room. You can imagine the sight I must have made: jacket, no shirt; trousers and shoes, but no socks. I walked up to the service desk and told the reservations clerk that I needed a room. The clerk was curt. "How long do you need the room?" I said, "I don't know. I don't know." He asked me, "Well, how long do you think you'll be staying?" I said, "A long time." He said, "I have to have two months' rent from you right now, in advance. That's 140 rands." Since I had no money, I just looked at him blankly. He looked at me, I looked back at him. It was obvious that there was going to be no transaction with this half-dressed 16-year-old. "I'm sorry," he said at last. "I can't help you."

I decided to see if my boss was still at the shop. Maybe he could help me come up with a plan. I left the hotel, ran the few blocks to Radio Hillbrow, and to my relief, Mr. Grant was still in the shop working on a display. He looked me over with a quizzical and worried expression and asked me what was up. I began blabbering about my situation, about how my mother wouldn't even let me put on a shirt, and I didn't have my front-door key anymore, and the unreasonable reservations clerk who was demanding two months' rent. And with every word, I became more and more unglued.

I continued through the full flight of my ramblings until I was exhausted and didn't know what else to say. I stared at Mr. Grant vacantly, not knowing what to do next. He walked straight to the cash register, took 140 rands out of the till, and placed it in my hand. He didn't ask me how or where or when I was going to pay him back. He didn't ask me how he could be sure I wasn't going to rip him off. He just said, "Here, I'll see you tomorrow," and handed me the money.

Triumphantly, I returned to the hotel, paid the snotty clerk, and was led to my room, which was in the basement level at the rear of the building. The room had a bed with sheets and one paper-thin blanket, a small sink, a closet, and a strip of window looking up to a parking space behind the hotel. The clerk left and I sat motionless on the side of the tiny bed for what seemed like an eternity, trying unsuccessfully to make sense of things and feeling pretty lonely.

Then I remembered the little radio that I had in my jacket pocket. I'll never forget that radio as long as I live. A birthday gift from my parents, it was a special miniature model designed and manufactured in Japan. It was the size of a matchbox, with an even tinier speaker. I popped it onto the nightstand beside the bed, turned up the volume as high as it would go, got into bed shivering under the thin blanket, and listened to the little squawking radio, because I needed the comfort and the company, and the radio provided me with both.

A NATURAL ABILITY TO LISTEN

I repaid Mr. Grant every cent by working extra hours. As the months went by, I found myself studying the man who had so unconditionally given me the money I needed. What was it about this guy? At first, all I could come up with was that he had human understanding without conditions, without criticism or judgement or strings attached. And it wasn't just with me, but with his wife and kids, who loved him beyond measure, and with his customers. He was doing something, and he was doing it consciously. I could sense it, but I couldn't quite identify it.

Then one day a farmer came into the shop looking for a new radio. He began to speak to Mr. Grant, and as he spoke I began to feel sorry for my boss. The farmer had a pronounced speech impediment, and I couldn't make out a single word he was saying. Poor Mr. Grant, I thought. He'll have to ask this man question after question in order to get the answers he needs to help the customer find what he's looking for.

To my amazement, in a couple of minutes the two of them were laughing as they walked around the store looking at radios. Mr. Grant would point one out and talk about it, the farmer would utter some indecipherable sounds, then Mr. Grant would respond with a comment. I realized that the two men were having a good old time carrying on a conversation. I was dumbstruck. So I angled myself closer to them, pretending to straighten items on a nearby shelf. I wanted to hear what

Mr. Grant was hearing. I strained and strained and recognized the model names of some of the radio sets. I was also pretty sure I heard him say "Frankenstein" and they both laughed.

The farmer chose a radio, paid for it, and left. Then it dawned on me. Mr. Grant was no miracle worker—he had an awesome ability to listen, and he listened with more precision and intensity than anyone I had ever known. Listening was a kind of tool for him. Then I remembered what he had told me a couple of years before: "I don't listen for what people need, I listen for what they want. That's how you build relationships in business and in life."

MR. GRANT'S OPEN EARS OPENED MY EYES

I had finally figured it out. Mr. Grant had a natural aptitude for listening, which he had honed into an awesome tool that helped his business survive and helped him build a network of people who cared for him deeply and who in turn made his life meaningful and pleasurable.

I tried to emulate Mr. Grant's listening skills, especially at the store. I also tried to copy his behaviour. I found that I was able to provide better service to customers and even helped boost sales by being a more effective salesman on the floor. More than this, I thought long and hard about the concept of adapting everyday skills into viable tools that I could use to enhance my life, whether it was to help build a business or to handle all kinds of situations in life.

I worked for Mr. Grant until I was 18 when I was drafted into the army. I emerged from those years with an insight into a new way to approach to life. I wasn't trying to become an entrepreneur like Mr. Grant. After all, at that time, my life revolved around the miseries that seemed to beset me on a regular basis. So my goals in life were to try to handle the tremendous anger that would well up within me, and the depths of sadness and hopelessness that accompanied it. I needed a way to cope. I needed a way to function effectively in the midst of my emotional upheavals. I needed a way to realign my emotions so that regardless of the intensity of my emotions, I would be able to use tools that would help me grow one powerful mind.

Journal Entry

Unconditional listening
is like
being warmed
by the sun on
a chilly day.

12

DISCOVERING THE
NATURAL FORCE OF REALIGNMENT

It is amazing how our minds work, how we latch on to something and won't let it go until it makes sense to us. That is what it was like for me as I thought about how Mr. Grant focused his natural listening ability to strengthen his relationships with his customers, with his family, and with me. Thus began a period of inner questioning that yielded me new insights into the patterns and processes of nature. This introspection showed me how a focused system of natural skills could transform life.

NATURE REALIGNS ITSELF, WHATEVER THE OUTCOME

I noticed a very simple but fascinating thing: when something in nature shifts out of alignment, it very soon establishes a new balance. Nature is in a constant state of realignment. It will always ensure adjustment and correction and balance. And it happens whether we like it or not. For example, when the northern hemisphere tilts away from the sun, the temperature turns cooler. Nature balances itself: trees shed their leaves and store their energy as sap for the winter, and birds migrate to warmer southern climates. The force of gravity keeps the earth orbiting the sun, and the forces of nature keep the trees producing sap and keep birds finding their way south. It is a peaceful system that has repeated itself year after year for aeons, a system whose components have remained constant for aeons.

Nature's process of realignment can also be destructive. For example, monsoons provide the water needed for the survival of certain flora and fauna in many near-tropical regions. At the same time, though, these rains often cause extensive damage and destruction to habitats. Hurricanes, forest fires, and floods generate the same combination of destruction and new order of growth. The components that are not strong enough to endure eventually are eliminated. As nature realigns, it nearly always transforms as it regains balance. Scientists believe, for example, that 165 million years ago, a large asteroid collided with Earth, generating a firestorm that wiped out many species of plants and animals. When the heat subsided, millions of other species perished as a consequence of the thick global dust cloud caused by the impact of the blast that shut out the sun's light and produced a severe period of killing cold.

Nevertheless, once again nature realigned itself. Giant species such as the dinosaur became extinct, while smaller species such as hominids, and eventually humans, took their place. The forces of nature had realigned the components of life and established a new natural order. Nature's correction did not care that some species were going to live and some were going to die. Nature's only function was to constantly realign itself, whether that outcome spelled survival or destruction for the species on Earth.

Today, the forces of nature are at work realigning the components of life and establishing a new natural order largely as a consequence of human input. The earth's ozone layer, for example, is degenerating largely as a result of the chemical compounds humans release into the atmosphere. Similarly, the climate is realigning itself to the effects of our production of greenhouse gases. The result is a steady increase in the earth's overall atmospheric temperatures. How will natural forces realign now? Again, the ecosystems will alter, as it has started to already. Sooner than we think, these natural forces of realignment and correction will affect our lives in ways about which we can only speculate.

The fact remains, these natural forces will create realignment and a new balance that will make some species flourish and that will destroy others. And whether we like the results or not, the system will not change. In time, nature will always realign itself to regain its harmony. What cannot withstand the correction will fall away and be replaced by something that can. This is the system of natural balance. It is inherent and powerful.

NATURE REALIGNS OUR PERSONAL LIVES, WHATEVER THE OUTCOME

As in nature, it is our human nature to realign our lives and establish balance.

Often, the realignments are peaceful and nurturing. You are hungry, so you eat; you are tired, so you rest. You need a roof over your head and a car and vacations and nice clothes, so you work for a living. You need to complete a difficult task at work, so you solicit the help of others to assist you. Each time, you follow a natural system of action that meets your needs. You rely on a pattern of thought and action that operates as a system that leads to a resolution,

Just as often, however, in today's era of unparalleled stress and tension, the realignments we experience in our lives are tumultuous and destructive—to others and to ourselves. You don't know how to handle a co-worker, so you quit or get fired, and you're struggling to make ends meet. Your teenage child has become a discipline problem, so you kick him out and risk losing his love forever.

I could cite many more examples of the complex, emotionally charged situations that we attempt to realign using the all-reactive cavebrain. They all share one thing: not only does each situation involve thoughts and actions that operate as a system that leads to resolution, they also include the single wild-card factor that distinguishes the peaceful and nurturing realignment from the destructive realignment: cavebrain emotion. When cavebrain emotion factors into the realignment process, the cavebrain takes over and the realignment that results is nearly always painful.

Human beings rely on a pattern of thought and action that evolved thousands of years ago, a system that leads to resolution. But what if that system is struggling to realign itself? What if the stresses and dangers we face today were never intended to be sustained for periods longer than a few seconds? In the past, our abilities to cope relied on a system uniquely adapted to meet the demands of the time. In a contemporary milieu of sustained stress and tension, are we still responding in a manner that may be in sync with our ancestral past but out of sync with contemporary realities? Has the natural force of realignment caught up sufficiently to provide us with an alternative way of reacting?

We are currently struggling to balance the demands of modern life with the reactions of the past. We are dominated by the cavebrain. And when cavebrain reactions of the past meet the complex demands of the present, our natural balance is disturbed. Nature will correct itself in time, but we can help nature along to effect this change sooner.

HUMANKIND INFLUENCES ITS OWN OUTCOMES

One of the great distinguishing factor of humankind is its inherent determination to influence the circumstances of its own existence. The impressive scientific and technological advances of the 20th century allow us to observe how profoundly we can affect our own circumstances. The Human Genome Project, for example, will soon have mapped out and defined the nature and function of every human gene. This research has already led to gene therapies that are transforming health care worldwide. Modern robotics are enabling us to safely complete tasks that, previously, placed humans in highly dangerous positions.

We have focused our skills, talents, and energies with remarkable success. We demand higher standards of living, better standards of health, and improved standards of recreational pleasure. But how are we using our natural skills to enable us to reach higher standards of self-esteem, higher standards of personal accomplishment, and higher standards of interpersonal relations? What is the conscious system of natural skills that can realign our lives and enable us to achieve these standards?

As discussed earlier, one of the differences between our ancestral civilization and today's is that in our cave-dwelling days our need to manage our emotions was a comparatively less complex and less infrequent requirement. Today, the demand to manage our emotions has become constant as we struggle with modern pressures. We need to learn to manage them if we want to achieve the goals that modern times demand. Allowing the cavebrain to run rampant puts us out of sync with our natural desire for personal growth.

We find it increasingly difficult, however, to tame the cavebrain, to engage the natural rhythms of life, the natural cycles of growth and change, and renewal and rebirth. It is so hard for us because we are forced to cope with a constantly shifting and increasingly pressured urban environment which has heightened the activity of our cavebrain reactions. It has also heightened the need to manage those reactions.

Our psychological needs are just as important as our physical needs, which is one of the reasons that we need a system of natural skills that is as consciously focused and effective as the systems used by scientists and engineers who make our physical lives so much more manageable. It is time that we help ourselves manage our emotions. Let me say it once more: it is the nature of humankind to realign itself and find a new balance. Most important, it is the nature of humankind to influence its own outcomes, including its capacity to manage emotions. Through this awareness, we assist and consequently enhance this natural process. These insights were, for me, tremendous revelations. They made me realize that we have everything we need to develop a system that could effectively integrate our rational with our emotional capacities.

THE EMOTIONAL MANAGEMENT SYSTEM

The Emotional Management System is a natural process of managing your own outcomes. It is a defined system of natural tools that helps you to consciously realign your emotional and rational capacities in order to achieve a Position of Independence, the new state of awareness and power you gain when you learn to apply the Emotional Management System.

Every step in the system is a natural skill, from the first step, STOPPING, which is a natural instinctive process, to the other six steps—listening, researching, considering your own opinion, considering the pros and cons of courses of action, and knowing where you want to go then going there.

These are all completely natural human skills. They aren't wild new psychological concepts and they aren't unique. The Emotional Management System is a conscious coping system that integrates emotional and rational capacities in a systematic way. This system of perfect natural processes is key in balancing the unnatural chaos we face in the stunningly pressurized world we live in.

These natural, instinctive processes must be allowed to operate in harmony with one another in order for each to work effectively. Change the dynamic of the whole and you weaken the system. If you remove one of the components from the system, you generate outcomes that are equally unbalanced and unstable. You cannot expect a stable result if you omit one of the prime components of the system.

THE CORE OF WITZ TRAINING

The period of introspection that led me to my insights about natural systems became my life's work. I continued to study everyday skills and noticed how people honed them into precise and effective life tools. I isolated these skills, examined how they functioned, then integrated them into seven distinct natural skills that form a system to help people achieve balance during times of emotional challenge.

Today, my early fascination with natural systems has grown to become a set of training courses. The Emotional Management System is a simple, powerful, and complete approach that has been assimilated and applied by more than 10,000 people over more than 20 years. It continues to be refined and learned year after year.

Journal Entry

Great ideas come
from great minds.
Brilliant ideas come
from
innocence.

13

SEVEN COMMON SKILLS INTEGRATED

The Emotional Management System provides a step-by-step approach to integrating your cavebrain with your computerbrain. It is a remarkably uncomplicated system, easily understandable, and instantly powerful. The sooner you assimilate it, the sooner you can learn to be self-sufficient, self-reliant, and balanced.

One of the hallmarks of the Emotional Management System is its logic. Consider the simplicity of this seven-step system:

Step 1:   **STOP** The first reaction of inner worth

Step 2:   **Listen** The conscious commitment to tune in

Step 3:   **Research** The power to distinguish the factual from the emotional

Step 4:   **Update Your Opinion** The factual integration of new thought

Step 5:   **Weigh the Pros and Cons** The wisdom to recognize the destination

Step 6:   **Define Your Objective** The freedom to control the direction you take

Step 7:   **GO** The alignment is complete

Each step in the Emotional Management System is a simple skill that you already use with near-total ease in most non-emotional situations every day. That is precisely why the system works so perfectly: these skills are an organic part of your life. The transformative power of these steps lies in their interdependence as each strategically allows your computerbrain to integrate with your cavebrain. The Emotional Management System is a progressive series of conscious wedges that keeps the door open between your cavebrain and computerbrain when the door attempts to shut.

Let's test the process. Consider a typical visit to the bank to order cheques, and you will see how naturally you use the skills that comprise the Emotional Management System.

Bank Teller: Is the chequebook you want to order for company or personal use?
You: Company.
Bank Teller: Would you like each chequebook to contain 50 or 100 cheques?
You: One hundred, please.
Bank Teller: One or two cheques per page?
You: Two per page, I think. What's the difference?
Bank Teller: It's a personal preference. Some people find two per page more convenient.
You: Okay, leave it at two per page.
Bank Teller: Now, cheque design. There are these to chose from [the teller shows you some samples]. You may want to keep the cheque as simple as possible like these, or try one of these.

Could you identify the steps?

Before you can answer the teller's question, you have to STOP. Even if it is only for a millionth of a second, you have to STOP.

Before you can answer the teller's question, you have to listen to it and understand what you have listened to. If the teller said something to you in a language you did not understand, such as "*Sawubona. Unjani wena? Usaphila na?* [which means, in the Zulu language, "Hello, How are you? Are you still well?"] you can hardly answer with "One hundred, please."

Although one of the steps in the Emotional Management System is "listen," this example illustrates that the process of merely listening to dialogue in and of itself is useless if you don't comprehend exactly what you are hearing.

You have listened but not understood what has been said. Therefore, you have to STOP (Step 1), listen and comprehend (Step 2). Let's follow the rest.

Bank Teller: One or two cheques per page?
You: Two per page, I think. What's the difference?

You initially allow your own opinion to be introduced. You have done no research. You will STOP (Step 1), albeit subconsciously, and for a millionth of a second. Then, having listened (Step 2), you stop, then research (Step 3). The interaction will be different:

Bank Teller: It's a personal preference really. Some people find it more convenient.
You: Hmm. Two would be a bigger book, but it would actually be easier for me to write on, I think. And that's what I'm after. So let's leave it at two per page.

After STOPPING twice, listening, and researching, you then bring in your own preference; in other words, your own updated opinion (Step 4). Then you weigh the pros and cons (Step 5) of choosing the two-cheques-per-page option, you define your objective (Step 6), which is to have a larger and easier surface to write on, and finally you proceed with your plan (Step 7) and select the two-cheques-per-page option.

In the above interaction, you have used every step in the Emotional Management System. You used this natural process in a simple harmonious balance of computerbrain and cavebrain. In fact, there was no emotion to indulge the dominating influence of the cavebrain. There was no emotion to generate the level of stress that could lead to confrontation or withdrawal, which would keep you from achieving your goal.

The system components as shown in the example above appear so stunningly simple precisely because they *are* simple. You use them perfectly many times each day. What you want to achieve, however, is to use the seven steps together during emotionally charged times. Combining the steps enables you to bypass your cavebrain's reactions. That is the true power of the system.

The Emotional Management System will teach you how to test your perceptions, decipher what you hear and see, as opposed to what you *think* you hear and see, gain control, and learn how to overcome obstacles. You will learn to control your thoughts and reactions, not suppress them. You will understand how to effectively deal with all the aspects of your life that bring emotions into the equation.

CREATING YOUR POSITION OF INDEPENDENCE

Independence, self-reliance and self-respect emerge when you have an emotional management system to follow. It affords you intellectual independence from the manacling effects of cavebrain-mode thinking. It lets you achieve emotional independence from the self-destructive momentum of unwarranted low self-esteem. It is the natural counterbalance you desperately need when life presents challenges that threaten to pull you down. It gives you the peace of mind you want and deserve. And it gives you the power to harmonize each facet of your life into a manageable and satisfying collage of experience.

Achieving a Position of Independence (PI) is not about denying your feelings or excusing them or avoiding them. That would be impossible. It is about realigning your emotions by connecting your emotional reactions with logical solutions. After all, you cannot stop yourself from experiencing a full range of emotions, and why would you? Emotions helps us to appreciate the full richness and colour of human existence.

THE SYNERGY OF THE SYSTEM

As you study the seven steps of the Emotional Management System that enable you to attain your Position of Independence, you will initially be examining each step in isolation. When you begin to apply the system, there will be times when the steps assume a natural, rhythmic flow as they rapidly lead one into another; at other times, some steps may take hours, even weeks, to complete and your progress may appear to be painstaking.

At first, you may find it difficult to understand how all seven steps in the system work in unison to bring your emotions into alignment. Don't be discouraged if this happens. As you learn each step and become familiar with the entire Emotional Management System, your understanding of the combined power of the seven steps will become crystal clear.

Journal Entry

Conditioning
is
an essential norm.

STEP 1: STOP—
THE FIRST REACTION OF INNER WORTH

Ironically, the step that makes the Emotional Management System go is the step that makes you STOP. Intuitively, you understand the importance of STOPPING. You know that you should STOP when you become aware that you are not helping yourself by going on. Have you ever tried to push open the door of an office building, but it doesn't budge? What do you do? You stop pushing. Then you notice that the door handle says "pull" so you pull the door open and in you go. We have all done that, and we have all managed to stop ourselves from trying to open the door the wrong way once we recognize why the wrong way doesn't work. You never even thought about it; you stopped, figured out what was happening, then made the right move.

When your cavebrain dominates your consciousness, your ability to stop yourself seems to disappear. And the fact is, when things go wrong, the most important action you can possibly take is to STOP. It's the kindest thing you can do for yourself; it's the most rewarding thing you can do for yourself. And it often feels like the toughest thing you can do. Why? Because it is the opposite of what your cavebrain is prompting you to do.

The problem is in this step's simplicity. STOPPING seems so obvious and so annoyingly elementary that we dismiss its importance. Rest assured, STOPPING is a critical step in the process of realigning your emotions. How do you measure the value of STOPPING? Well, when it comes to the big money and the big emotions, people have indeed placed a monetary value on STOPPING, and it serves as a marvellous model for explaining what seems to be a no-brainer.

Circuit Breakers—How Stock Exchanges Intentionally Stop

Stock exchanges around the world have adopted the STOP concept to minimize the negative effects of decision making founded on cavebrain-dominated emotional input. In the international investment world, major stock exchanges such as the New York Stock Exchange, the Toronto Stock Exchange, and the London Stock Exchange have developed systems called circuit breakers to manage and control the kind of panic buying and selling created by investors' runaway cavebrains. Circuit breakers are an ideal model for the STOP concept.

Computers at these stock exchanges monitor trading volumes and prices on each exchange. When overall market selling reaches a critical level of volume and price that reflects a market-panic profile (cavebrain reactions), the computerized circuit breakers kick in and trading is halted for a period of time. Investment decisions are not permitted to be executed until that period has elapsed.

The circuit breaker forces investors to STOP and gather more facts before making as genuinely an independent investment decision as possible. This system of STOPPING the momentum works remarkably well. It helps re-establish the opportunity for emotional equilibrium and independent position that supports people in making sound decisions.

STOP AND INVEST IN YOUR EMOTIONAL ALIGNMENT

I have been using and advocating the use of the STOP concept for more than two decades because it works. Consider the tremendous amount of emotion you invest during your life. When those emotions begin to spiral out of control, what can you do? You don't have a computer-assisted regulator when your cavebrain hijacks your emotions. But you do have a computerbrain structure (your neocortex) which you can train to intervene when the panic mode takes over.

Your experiences have likely shown you that the more powerful your emotions are, the more precarious the balance between intelligence and feelings. But you can indeed STOP your cavebrain. I like to think of this action as a neurophysical trigger. Just as stock exchange systems say STOP, so too can your computerbrain issue a STOP command to your runaway cavebrain. Issue the STOP command and you will be giving yourself the time to let your computerbrain initiate the ability to integrate its advanced thought with your strong emotions so that you can establish your Position of Independence.

What Does STOPPING Achieve?

STOPPING allows you to put your cavebrain reactions on pause long enough for you to connect to your computerbrain's input so that you can begin realigning your emotions. Once you create that pause, you create the opportunity for rational thought to align with emotion. STOPPING drives the wedge that allows your computerbrain to integrate with your cavebrain. When you STOP, you can introduce a rational perspective and alternatives, question perspectives, and begin the process of reaching your Position of Independence.

It is important for you to remember that you are not trying to STOP your emotions. You are trying to STOP your cavebrain from overpowering you.

Prove You Are Not a Robot

We are so accustomed to reacting automatically to our cavebrain reactions that we don't usually recognize that our aligned cavebrain-computerbrain thinking processes have shifted out of alignment and have become cavebrain-dominated. It happens all the time. For example, your spouse forgets to pick up the groceries and you automatically lash out in anger, losing all perspective on the situation. Or your boss leaves a message that she wants to see you and you're plagued by negative perceptions and expectations about what you believe is about to happen to you. Or your 15-year-old daughter is three-quarters of an hour late from her first date and you are paralyzed with fear. You feel helpless as a wave of panic overwhelms you.

Cavebrain reactions will almost certainly take over at some point in the above scenarios, and dictate decisions that at the time appear justified. Regardless of the emotion you feel, your cavebrain prompts you to react automatically, quickly, mindlessly, like a robot. But you are not a robot. You are an intelligent human being and your emotions are far too important to relegate to the automatic reaction patterns of the cavebrain. They deserve to be processed in a way that enables you to achieve the goals that will enhance your life. These intense reactions need to be controlled. Give yourself that opportunity to do so now. STOP.

STOP Means Stop

How do you STOP? Most people try to STOP by visualizing a big red stop sign. Others shout out the word in their heads. Whichever method works for you, the simple act of thinking STOP is enough to trigger the process.

Practise the stop sign visualization for a moment. What do you do when you're driving and come to a stop sign? You do what you have been conditioned to do: you stop, check the road for obstacles or oncoming traffic then prepare to proceed in your chosen direction. Not surprisingly, visualizing a stop sign is the simplest method for halting the chaotic momentum of your cavebrain and its attendant jumble of emotions. When you STOP, you trigger the rational mind, you don't set off a reactive response. This self-command is a neurophysical process that encourages you to pause long enough to initiate your moving to a Position of Independence.

STOP means stop. It is a simple directive and you can use it any time you want. It's not rocket science and you won't find scholars expounding on its intricacies and subtleties. It's a simple concept: STOP. STOP means stop. STOP. STOP.

To begin the process of realigning your emotions, you must manage to stop the chaotic momentum of misaligned emotions. You must STOP every thought and every emotion. You must STOP long enough to recognize that you have to tackle your situation from a rational perspective.

WATCHING THE STOP PERFORM

Nurit is a very kind person who could never say no to anyone who asked a favour of her. One morning Nurit was in the mall, running an errand for a colleague and running late in the process. She started to get very angry with her colleague for taking advantage of her good nature. Why does he always do this to me? she thought. He's just using me. He never does things for himself. He always gets other people to do things for him. He's selfish and I'm a fool for letting him ruin my day.

Nurit's anger was building and building. By the time she returned from the mall, she was in a rage. "I think I could actually feel the steam starting to come out of my ears," she told the group at the training session later. She was ready to storm over to her colleague's office and berate him for always forcing her to disrupt her schedule by asking her to do his infuriating errands.

It was at this point that Nurit, who had just learned about the Position of Independence and STOP concept, remembered to STOP. She told the group what a revelation it was. Once she STOPPED, she was able to apply her emotional management system. Without it, she realized that she was listening to her own opinion governed by her cavebrain voice, which was causing her intense reaction. She remembered that, unchecked, the cavebrain voice can be a damaging force as it is saturated with opinion and emotion and contains very little logic.

Nurit was able to conclude that her colleague was not at fault. After all, she was the one who had offered to help in the first place. In future, she would not jump in so quickly and volunteer to do his errands. Or if she was asked to do something and it was not convenient, she would say no.

She now says that while this was her initiation into the realm of the Position of Independence, she would never have been able to act from her PI had she not silently shouted out STOP to herself first.

Nurit no longer feels that people take advantage of her. She now does things on her terms. If she wants to say no, she does. If she want to say yes, she does so from a new point of inner strength. She has given herself a choice—a perfect Position of Independence.

Knee-jerk Reactions Make You Look Like a Jerk

There is no rule that states that you must react immediately to situations. In the case described above, Nurit enabled herself to reach her Position of Independence by STOPPING herself from acting on her inner reaction. Most of us, however, believe that we must demonstrate our intelligence with a think-on-your feet reaction.

I am always surprised by people who tell me they want to learn to think quicker on their feet. This has never been a goal of mine, nor a facility that I particularly admire. Thinking quickly is not the skill that improves life most. The skill that improves life most is the capacity to think more clearly. Thinking at a slower, more even pace is consistent with the concept of emotional management.

Ironically, knee-jerk reactions usually reveal lack of discipline and subjugation to your cavebrain's knee-jerk emotions. If you really want to display your intelligence, keep yourself from automatically following your cavebrain's suggestions. Instead, establish a PI so that you can remove the contamination caused by emotion, prejudice, and preconception and thus begin to gain genuine insight into and control of your situation.

STOP Does Not Mean Counting to Ten

One of my students once asked me if STOP is the same as stopping and counting to ten. It isn't.

Many of us have been taught to use that ploy to try to eliminate over-powering emotions—usually anger. It is an attempt to prevent the momentum of the cavebrain. The count-to-ten approach holds that by the time you have counted slowly to ten, any strong emotions you are feeling will have dissipated and you will be able to think clearly and make effective and astute decisions. Well, that's great if the source of your concern dissipates as well. But that rarely happens.

Since the source of your concern remains, counting to ten does little to help you deal with the cavebrain reactions that inevitably ensue. The stresses that lead us to make our self-sabotaging decisions are created by a build-up of pressures. To simply count to ten is to put off the inevitable self-destructive explosion. There is no system or solution following the count. In my opinion, counting to ten is a waste of ten seconds.

STOP is not a waste of time, however. It works. It is the first step in a powerful series of easy-to-learn and easy-to-maintain steps that put you back in control.

STOP IS A TRIGGER DEVICE

STOPPING triggers the entire realignment process. It is a mini management system that establishes your PI. This neurophysical trigger device enables you to cap your automatic cavebrain reaction. You may react spontaneously for a certain period of time, but once you are able to STOP, you create the pause to step back and initiate or activate a system that allows you to integrate the rational computerbrain into the equation. This system takes some understanding, true, and there are steps and procedures you will learn easily, but advanced emotional management only works when you begin by STOPPING.

STOPPING Means Interrupting Yourself

When you STOP, you interrupt your emotions and impulses and allow yourself to move into the system which ultimately gives you more control over your feelings. You want this trigger to become a subconscious habit. Initially, it takes enormous effort to interrupt yourself long enough to STOP going in the wrong direction. But once you practise the process, it quickly becomes an effective and rewarding habit.

STOPPING Helps You Go

STOP prevents you from being overrun by your cavebrain reactions and affords your rational mind the chance to listen logically to your perceived emotion or fear. You are the only one who can give your computerbrain the opportunity to merge with your cavebrain and benefit from the integration of emotion and intellect.

STOPPING Doesn't Mean Avoiding

Nurit learned to STOP and then determine an appropriate response to her interpersonal challenge. She recognized her cavebrain reactions to help her computerbrain find a solution.

Unfortunately, many people believe they have acted from their Position of Independence if they have managed to suppress the intense emotions they are experiencing. Suppressing emotion does not eliminate their influence. Suppressing emotion is tantamount to putting your feelings into a pressure cooker. Their influence will become stronger as more feelings accumulate. Your feelings will become increasingly mixed and confusing. Ultimately these unresolved emotions will seek an alternate outlet.

You cannot control whether or not you have feelings, but you *can* control what you do with them, and how long they last. This is what emotional management is all about: being smart about your emotions and using them to help, not hurt, yourself.

STOPPING Means Defusing Your Cavebrain

When you STOP reacting, you give yourself an opportunity to consider choice. This choice gives you freedom. You will find that you no longer say to yourself, "I can't." You say, "Let me find another way. Let me analyze the situation. Let me introduce an intelligent, logical, and rational approach." You are effectively ordering yourself to take responsibility, and it all starts simply by letting yourself STOP. You are achieving self-reliance. You are achieving a Position of Independence.

The STOP concept is so powerful because it is the first reaction of inner worth. You are going to forge your own freedom and stop being victimized by the unreasonable demands others place upon you or that you place upon yourself.

STOPPING HELPS YOU STAND UP FOR YOURSELF

A student of mine has a boss that used to bully him. Gordon's boss, Stan, had mistreated him for three and a half years, and Gordon didn't know how to deal with him. A few years ago, Gordon accidentally omitted an essential product chart from an important business proposal and his company lost the contract.

Stan, who was well aware of the omission, ordered Gordon into his office, shut the door, and launched into a tirade. Gordon naturally felt a mixture of anger and fear, but instead of retreating from this bully, he simply STOPPED. Still berating Gordon, Stan advanced on him and tried to force him to step back in submission. Where Gordon would have retreated in the past, he actually STOPPED. He moved to the chair in front of Stan's desk, sat down, crossed his legs comfortably, and looked back at Stan blankly, showing no emotion and making no attempt to react.

Gordon's STOPPING incited Stan even more. He began to scream and pound his fist on the desk, his eyes popping out of his head. The confrontation ended as suddenly as it began. Stan stopped yelling abruptly, looked at Gordon for a second, then turned and stormed out of his own office, and out of the building.

Gordon called me the next day, saying, "I'm very confused. This morning the guy was as nice as a lamb to me." Of course he was. Stan realized he'd lost it. He'd made a fool of himself and then he was embarrassed. He had crossed over the boundary of acceptable professional behaviour.

Stan had learned that intimidation was not going to generate a reaction in Gordon any longer. Gordon still works for Stan, and Stan treats Gordon quite differently. It was the classic bully syndrome. You STOP and refuse to let yourself react in fear and anger and the bully feels powerless and soon leaves you alone. All Gordon did, to begin to respond effectively, was

STOP. By STOPPING, Gordon contrasted his computerbrain's composed approach with Stan's primal, cavebrain, out-of-control reaction.

Gordon didn't conform to the typical reactive behaviours most of us follow when faced by an intimidating situation. A cool head almost always prevails over a hot-headed reaction. The most important thing for you to understand is that STOPPING allows you to initiate your Position of Independence. Your emotional management system allows you to control your instant reactions. You STOP so that you can trigger your integrated cavebrain-computerbrain process. When your computerbrain is integrated, *you* control your objectives, as opposed to being controlled by your emotions or someone else's.

Gordon did not know what would happen after he STOPPED, but look what actually did happen. STOPPING changed the pattern of interaction that Stan was familiar with. Stan did not receive the reactive cues from Gordon that would allow Stan to conform to his usual pattern, so suddenly Stan was out of sync, forced to pay attention to Gordon, not because of Gordon's emotional reactions, but because of the *absence* of them. Gordon demonstrated a quality that Stan had not encountered before, which effectively ended the interaction. In the end, Stan was merely yelling at himself. So, by restructuring the interaction, Gordon initiated the respect process.

By STOPPING, Gordon eliminated an unpleasant reactive pattern with his boss. However, nothing improved over the long term just because Gordon STOPPED. If that was all you and I and the Gordons of the world had to do, the Emotional Management System would comprise but one step. Gordon improved the relationship with Stan by building on the success of STOPPING and following through with the remaining steps in the Emotional Management System, beginning with Step 2: Listen.

15

STEP 2: LISTEN—THE CONSCIOUS
COMMITMENT TO TUNE IN

Listening is the skill that allows you to focus your attention on the world around you. Your computerbrain is engineered to use the natural skill of listening, to open you to your world. In fact, the brain is far more effectively designed to listen to words than to try to produce them. The brain can process four times as many words it is listening to than it is trying to say. But when you are riding a wave of cavebrain reactions, your mind is usually concentrating on the singular source of threat. It makes sense: your survival depends on your not being distracted.

You will gain a lot more by listening than by concentrating solely with a cavebrain ear with its singular motive—survival. In the bigger picture, the survival motive alone is a pretty inefficient use of your brain. Think about all the information you process when you listen. Calmly listening to and considering all the facts helps you resolve an array of issues. You can hear important information that can alter negative perceptions you are holding on to—perceptions that, until you listen carefully, may have held you back.

THE AWESOME POWER OF WORDS

Words have the power to thrill your soul or devastate you completely. Think about how important words are to you. Think about how easily you become confused or hurt or delighted by what you thought you heard. This is the power of words.

It would seem patently unwise to allow yourself to be affected by words that you are not certain you actually heard but only assume you heard. Unfortunately, however, we do it all the time. This phenomenon is a symptom of cavebrain thinking which creates emotional reactions often without verifying the data it is basing these reactions upon. In this way you become a slave to your cavebrain, and the consequences are usually stressful, if not disastrous. When you STOP (Step 1), you give yourself the opportunity to actually listen and verify the verbal data your brain is processing.

During emotionally charged situations, you need your total capacity to listen. But when emotions intrude, you use your listening skills the least. The cavebrain is busy applying its awesome survival motive and so redirects all your attention to the single source that threatens you. To solve the problem, you need to focus on listening. Therefore, you must counteract the cavebrain's reactions with a strong computerbrain response. By counterbalancing your cavebrain's singular focus, you regain your ability to use your full listening ability.

YOU HEAR BUT DO YOU LISTEN?

Each of us believes that we actually listen. When I talk about the need to listen, be aware that you may think that you are listening carefully, but in fact the odds are stacked against you. As soon as you hear something you do not like to hear or with which you disagree, you likely shift from an aligned cavebrain-computerbrain information processing system to an internal cavebrain mode. Your listening has shifted out of alignment. You begin to listen to your thoughts instead of what is being said, and if your emotions are at an intense level, it is unlikely that your computerbrain is controlling your listening.

The fact is, we get confused between the process of hearing and the process of listening. There are distinct differences between the two. Hearing is a sensory function. It is an instinctive process: you hear whether you are inclined to or not. Listening, on the other hand, is an elective process. You select what you want to hear.

Hearing Things

Walter attended his office party at the home of one of his co-workers. He had too much to drink and decided to call a cab to take him home. Walter stepped into the kitchen to use the phone. As he hung up, the phone cord caught the edge of the counter and knocked his wineglass onto the floor, where it broke. Justin, his host, was annoyed and reprimanded Walter.

The next day Walter apologized to Justin only to find himself further criticized by Justin for behaving inappropriately. Two weeks later, Walter was sipping beer at a sports bar up the street from his office, when Justin walked in, approached Walter, and said, "What are you drinking this time?" Walter immediately responded, "What? You think I'm going to get sloshed again?"

Walter had not listened. He only heard what he thought Justin was implying. He interpreted Justin's statement as implying that he was drinking too much again and that he was going to lose control and make a fool of himself. Because Walter was sensitive about having been criticized for drinking too much at the party, and was embarrassed by the event, he allowed his perceptions to create their own facts, completely independent of Justin's actual words.

It never really occurs to any of us that we can hear—as loudly as we hear actual words—what we believe is being implied. Even though the actual words are never uttered, we hear what we think is said through the filter of our cavebrain's protectionist survival motive. Many of us get into terrible predicaments because we fail to distinguish what was actually said from what our cavebrain believes it heard by implication. We end up listening not to the message delivered through someone's words, but to the message delivered by our own thoughts about what we conclude is the implied message.

Justin never did finish his conversation with Walter. Perhaps if he had, Walter might have heard, "What are you drinking this time?" followed by "I think I'll have one." Justin's message had nothing to do with criticism. It turned out simply to be a question: "What are you drinking?"

Jumping to Conclusions

Misperceptions, like the one described above, occur all the time. Here is another example. I was delivering a lecture a year ago about dealing with difficult people, when an elderly couple asked me how to handle a situation they'd found themselves in. Here's their story:

The woman's husband claimed that his neighbour was always angry with him. When I asked how he knew that this was so, he said that he could tell because the man would clear his throat before he spoke.

I asked him if he was putting me on, but he assured me that he wasn't. The man told me that he used to work for an extremely dominating, critical, and intimidating boss who constantly reprimanded him. Before he did so, however, the boss always cleared his throat.

This throat-clearing became an indication that a reprimand would always follow. The man's neighbour had the unfortunate habit of regularly clearing his throat. As a result, regardless of what was actually said to the old gentleman, he believed he was hearing a reprimand. He would then argue with his neighbour, who argued back, thus reinforcing the man's belief that his neighbour was on a never-ending campaign to intimidate him.

As I listened to the man's story, I noticed that he regularly cleared his throat. I asked him if he was annoyed with me. He insisted that of course he wasn't. I pointed out that in fact he had just cleared his throat. The incredulous look he delivered was the catalyst he needed and the opportunity for him to observe how easily his perceptions distorted reality.

Emotions and perceptions can make some very powerful statements. You have to learn to appreciate the distinction between listening openly and completely and hearing selectively. It's important to keep clear listening in the fore when cavebrain reactions draw your attention to your own thoughts instead of to the actual message being delivered.

LISTENING IS AN ACTIVE PROCESS

Listening, unlike hearing, is a selective, conscious process.

Active participative listening occurs when you actively and consciously listen. You listen, without interruption of thought, to what is being said. Easier said than done.

Active participative listening often leads to reflective listening. Reflective listening is listening to what you have already heard. Reflective listening is normally done when you are on your own, reviewing what you have heard in an interaction with someone. As in active participative listening, to truly listen reflectively you must be sure to restrict your own interpretations and opinions or analyses as much as possible. Again, easier said than done.

Don't let your opinions interrupt the interaction prematurely. They can produce some very corrosive perceptions. There is the right time to include your input, but when you haven't understood all the external information clearly, your own input will not give you a balanced perspective. Inserting your opinion prematurely means you've skipped a step in the process. At this point in the Emotional Management System you must keep the steps separate; otherwise, it is like adding a cup of flour to a cup of water, with four eggs tossed in for good measure all at once. The result, even though the essential ingredients are all there, is a lumpy mess.

Learning to Listen All Over Again

The most expedient way to corrupt the listening process is to believe you actually are listening. You will not improve your listening skills if you assume that you listen well without being truly aware of whether you are, in fact, listening.

Here's a great little test you can use to evaluate someone's listening skills. Read a short paragraph to someone. Don't tell them why, and move the conversation in another direction briefly, for a minute or so. Then quickly ask them to repeat in their own words what they thought you read to them moments ago. You will be both horrified and amazed by the results. You will understand with startling clarity how people are hearing you but not really listening.

This exercise might make you wonder how on earth we manage to achieve so much in life while listening to so little of what others say. Consider how many mistakes you are actually making by not listening to what is being said to you. As you improve your ability to listen, you are able to align your listening skills to the actual messages being delivered to you so you can establish your Position of Independence.

To successfully reach your PI you must first learn to fight your natural tendency to angle your listening in the direction of your own inner monologue, as well as your tendency not to listen at all when you don't like what you hear. Your PI will be instantly or seriously compromised if your perceptions encourage immediate disagreement with what you are hearing and if you allow your emotions to block your listening ability.

Consider how easily your perceptions focus on what you want to listen to. If you perceive that the person you are speaking with is stupid or doesn't understand you, your perception will not permit you to listen with a balanced view when they speak. Rather, you will judge what is being said by your perception of the person with whom you are speaking. Consequently, it is easy to discount what he or she says because the actual content of the dialogue contrasts with your interpreted point of view about that person. The reverse phenomenon applies equally frequently. I have seen people hanging on to every word and believing everything that was being said because they perceived the person to be an authority. They interpret everything they hear as totally factual, regardless of the actual facts.

Emotions Prevent Hearing from Becoming Listening

If you are sensitive and your self-esteem is low, your opinion about others during an interaction can wreak havoc on your ability to distinguish what is actually being said from what you think is being said. Similarly, if you feel that someone does not agree with you, your emotions will cloud your listening abilities in your efforts to justify that what he or she is saying is unfounded or irrelevant. You shut out as much as you can.

When you are intensely sensitive to the escalating emotions within you during a conversation, you are not particularly inclined to listen to what you are hearing. Consider the following:

You have lost your job as a salesperson because you have trouble following a prescribed sales method. You felt the approach was pushy, insincere, and unethical.

When you tell your wife that you lost your job, she says that some people just aren't cut out for that kind of sales position. She is actually attempting to frame a response that demonstrates her empathy. In your heightened emotional state, however, you are so intensely frustrated and angry at your situation and your former employer for firing you that you are consumed with the feeling of being persecuted.

So when your wife says that some people aren't cut out for that kind of sales position, your persecution-oriented emotions have you hear her say that you didn't know how to do your job, and you interpret that to mean that you are inept and a failure. Given your inability to do the job, you "hear" her say, you probably shouldn't be in sales, ever. You do not truly listen to what she said. Your cavebrain reaction immediately begins to counter the criticism you were certain you heard. In fact, no criticism was made at all.

Listening Stops When You Reach Your Emotional Wall

Typically we listen up to a point of disagreement. Prior to any disagreement, the cavebrain doesn't identify any inherent threat, so the listening is not corrupted. Once there is disagreement, we instantly come to our own conclusions without following the necessary steps that would enable us to arrive at a legitimately updated opinion.

It is amazing how startlingly self-absorbed people can become. Consider Britain's Prince Charles. In November 1997, just weeks after the tragic death of Diana, Princess of Wales, London's *Sunday Times* was one of a number of newspapers to report that former British prime minister John Major was working with a battery of lawyers trying to straighten out the legal and financial affairs of Prince William, then 15, and his 13-year-old brother, Prince Harry.

The media reported that there were complications concerning the princess's $46-million estate because she had not altered her will following her divorce from Prince Charles. According to news reports, her will had estimated her estate at $2.25 million. Charles discovered this loophole and demanded the return of the $38 million he'd given Princess Diana under the terms of their divorce agreement. Charles could also recoup any interest on that sum.

How does this story affect your opinion of Charles? Does he appear to be more insensitive and greedier than you may have initially thought? Are his actions the epitome of crassness, selfishness, and self-interest? It certainly appears that way, and it appears to confirm a popular opinion that Prince Charles is self-absorbed and detached, far removed from the realities of day-to-day life. This is how it appears, that is, until you hear the whole story.

As it turns out, Charles's motive was not to challenge the terms of the divorce agreement in order to benefit himself. His efforts were meant to benefit his two sons. If Prince Charles succeeded in overturning the divorce settlement, then placed the sum of $38 million, plus interest, into a trust administered on behalf of his two sons, he would save the two young princes from having to pay an enormous inheritance tax.

Due to massive public sympathy for Diana and equally massive worldwide condemnation for the treatment of the princess by the Royal Family, and specifically by Diana's apparently disinterested and unfaithful husband, Charles, we are already preconditioned to expect further selfish behaviour from the prince. Ultimately, however, by listening to all the facts, we realize that Prince Charles's motives were not selfish, but were entirely devoted to the interests of his two children, thus revealing a protective, paternal side to a man that popular opinion held to be cold and indifferent.

Only when you realize the need to engage your computerbrain can you begin to make optimal use of your listening skills. Without this ability, the untrained listener undermines his or her own goals. Now it is time to learn the right way to listen.

ARE YOU OVERLY CRITICAL OF CRITICISM?

Are you willing to listen to criticism that is levelled at you? You may respond that you are, as long as the criticism is constructive. In other words, *you* will determine if it is constructive or not. If you like what you hear, you may act on it. If, on the other hand, you don't like what you hear, you will disregard it. Is your cavebrain distorting your understanding of the situation and therefore your approach to it? Are you certain you don't dismiss some criticism as unconstructive because hearing it upsets you? If something is upsetting to you, does that automatically lead you to conclude that it is unconstructive? Can you afford to dismiss what you are hearing because it upsets you? Or because you don't like the delivery? Or because you don't like the deliverer? You may be dismissing the very observations that will generate the awareness you need for personal growth.

Listen to Everything

Learn to listen to everything that is being said. Accept that not everything you listen to will be what you want to hear. Be determined to listen. You have to make a conscious choice. Unless you listen to everything with a balanced view, you will have a tough time gaining a Position of Independence.

If you do not listen to everything, you will miss important information; you will miss essential content. Not everything you hear will be accurate. Not everything you hear you will like. The Emotional Management System is designed to help you distinguish between the facts and fictions you listen to.

Hear It Once, Repeat It Twice

When you listen, it is helpful to hear what is being said more than once, especially when you are receiving information that charges you up emotionally. You can achieve this by either repeating what you heard or by writing down the salient points. The more you engage your computer-brain, the more you will hear.

Listen to Bad News That Doesn't Concern You

Generally we find it easier to listen when we like what we hear or when there are no distractions. Such conditions make listening easy. You are open. The more difficult goal is to listen intently so you avoid imposing your cavebrain-dominated opinion, especially in situations in which you disagree.

But bad news is unpleasant. Insults are unpleasant. Complaints are unpleasant. Confrontations are unpleasant. They close you up inside and leave you listening less to what you are hearing and more to what you are feeling. In such cases you are not listening to what is being said, but to your own little internal voice—your opinion.

One of the most effective exercises to help you improve your listening skills is to note how other people listen. Tune in to a talk show on radio or TV. These broadcasts are loaded with emotionally charged conversations about myriad problems. You'll notice that the guests on these shows don't seem to listen to the words that the audience or host are saying to them about their situations. They physically hear what is being said to them, but they don't seem able to listen in a balanced way.

Why can't these people listen? When they feel attacked or insecure, they have difficulty listening because they are so gripped by their cavebrain reactions that they will not allow their computerbrains to integrate their critical and objective faculties into the process. Take two minutes during any one of these broadcasts to write down the most important things that were said to the troubled guests. Listen carefully. Don't try to pretend you are one of the emotional people on the panel. Simply note precisely what is being said.

This exercise will indicate how much you are able to listen compared to the participants who are personally involved. In those shows, questions go unanswered, people get stuck in their own opinions, and emotions distort what is said. This exercise will help you listen to these kinds of dialogue during interactions in which you *are* one of the participants. The better you become at listening in an emotional situation in which you have no direct involvement, the more you will recognize the need to listen in an emotional situation of your own.

WONDER AS YOU WANDER OFF IN THOUGHT

It is natural to wander off into your own thoughts during a conversation. Try to become aware of how often you do this. Once you realize that you are not focusing on the conversation, you have options.

You can:

1. Apologize to the person you're talking to and say, "I'm sorry I didn't quite catch that. Could you please say that again if you don't mind?" (People are generally uncomfortable saying that. I have heard people say something that is a non sequitur because they didn't hear what was said in the first place. In their attempt to appear to know what is going on, they make fools of themselves.)

2. Inform the person you're talking to that you would like clarification and could they please explain in more detail.

3. Inform the person you're talking to that you are having trouble focusing right now and ask if they could repeat what was said. Listening will naturally lead you to the next step in the Emotional Management System—Research.

Discover the value of listening. It will stand you in amazingly good stead.

A wise old man once told me something I have never forgotten. He said, "I know what it is I have to say but because I don't necessarily know what the person I'm talking with is going to say. I listen carefully. I have plenty of time to say what I want to say."

I wish I had said that.

STEP 3: RESEARCH—THE POWER TO DISTINGUISH THE FACTUAL FROM THE EMOTIONAL

Steps 1 (STOP) and 2 (Listen) of the Emotional Management System are difficult because their objective is to drive a wedge into the cavebrain's unilateral agenda and create a conscious bridge that allows your computerbrain to create healthy emotional intelligence. Step 3 (Research) capitalizes on the achievements of the first two steps by giving you the power to distinguish the factual from the emotional at those moments when you need to do this most: when you are working to establish the most emotionally intelligent pattern of thought you can. Achieving this step is a major turning point in the Emotional Management System. For the first time in the process, you are focusing almost entirely on the advanced capacity of your computerbrain. This is where you begin to truly manage your emotions and take control of your life. You are starting to use your brain instead of being used by it.

WHAT YOU USUALLY DO AFTER STOPPING AND LISTENING

When your cavebrain is dominating your behaviour, you don't use your computerbrain to carefully investigate the world around you (research). Instead, you instantly retrieve your preset opinions about your world in order to maintain momentum. That is why discovering your own opinion is not difficult. At times when your cavebrain is active, you retrieve your opinion immediately, even before you have heard all the facts. It is a reactive thought pattern, and when that pattern tells you that you already know something, you have no motivation to look further. The fact is, *you will not learn what you perceive you already know.* Your opinion is an essential part of establishing your Position of Independence, but it is useful only when it is genuinely informed, and that is where research is required to accurately update your opinion.

Many issues affect you emotionally. Allowing emotions to infiltrate, however, can interfere with your Position of Independence, which means you risk returning to the outcomes caused by cavebrain thinking. This is what usually occurs when you feel vulnerable, frustrated, annoyed, and so on. If you allow your emotions to infiltrate, you may find that you are using only Step 4 of the seven realignment steps. You are listening, yes, but to your own preconceived opinion. You believe you are researching, but your opinion has already decided what the facts are. In such a situation, you are not following the emotional management system, you are collapsing the seven steps into a single chain in the following pattern:

Step 1   (STOP) You have your own opinion, so you don't even recognize the need to STOP.

Step 2   (Listen) You listen to your own opinion, so you believe you *are* listening. Therefore you don't feel you need to listen any more than you already are.

Step 3   (Research) You "know" the facts. You consider your own opinion as a credible substitute for actual input, so you don't feel you need to research anything.

Step 4   (Update your opinion) Your own opinion is featured centre stage, reinforcing itself.

Step 5   (Weigh the pros and cons) There is nothing to contemplate. After all, you have already reached your conclusion, which took only an instant to form.

Step 6   (Define your objective) You define your objective based on your own untested opinion.

Step 7   (Go) You act, based on your cavebrain reaction, without having integrated your computerbrain input.

Typically, this process achieves unwanted and unintended results. You begin with your own opinion, you interact with your own opinion from every possible angle in order to give it as much credence as possible, then you act on it. Your cavebrain reactions, which have been out of alignment with your computerbrain's input, remain out of alignment. The connection has never been made. And you are no better off than you were.

It is difficult to eliminate the influence of your own opinion. I am not asking you to eliminate it; I am asking you to manage it. You will be serving your best interests if you wait in the wings a while longer as you gather more information about your situation. An opinion that is not fully informed can severely corrupt your Position of Independence. Research permits you to update your thoughts to widen your view so that you can act in a responsible manner that will serve not only your best interests, but also the interests of others who are also involved in the situation.

THE CAVEBRAIN DOES NOT WANT YOU TO RESEARCH ITS EMOTIONS

Research permits you to achieve a great deal but only if you are able to STOP (Step 1) and listen (Step 2), because your cavebrain reacts without thought. Remember, the cavebrain drives your survival instinct, and therefore there isn't much time for thought. The problem is, individuals rarely analyze a situation correctly when it is saturated with emotions. At these times, it is a contradiction in terms to "intellectually consider" your situation.

It is extremely difficult to behave rationally in an emotional situation. You react rather than think. This is a natural cavebrain behaviour. After all, the cavebrain's mandate is to act absolutely immediately, otherwise your very life may be in peril. So it is often natural for you to feel impelled to do something right away, which is to create a self-protective, self-centred, and quickly formed opinion, based on nothing but your own emotions. You form a strong opinion about either yourself or about the people you are interacting with, and these strong, uncontested opinions obstruct rational thought.

To illustrate this point, take, for example, racists. Racists are inflamed by their cavebrain preconceptions. People who are informed easily identify the racist's position as uninformed and inaccurate. Nevertheless, racists emphatically dismiss all rational objections to their views regardless of the evidence placed before them. I know of two professors who propagate the revisionist-history notion that the Holocaust never happened; it is merely, they insist, a masterful Jewish conspiracy of such magnitude and precision that historians have been intellectually incapable of disproving it. Despite all evidence to the contrary, these people actually believe their own rhetoric. All the arguing in the world cannot displace such prejudice. Perception equals fact. And inaccurate uninformed perceptions equal inaccurate uninformed facts.

THE BENEFITS OF RESEARCH

Research is vitally important to humankind, and it is vitally important to achieving balanced emotional intelligence. Research encourages a rational approach that finds you thinking, asking questions, looking for logical answers, and arriving at rational conclusions so that you can make the necessary connection between your cavebrain and your computerbrain.

Research allows you to look at options. It allows you to analyze the information you have gathered. Research helps prevent instant reactions. Through research you give yourself choices concerning how to act, when to act, and if to act at all. If you are to make positive changes in your life, if you are to decide for yourself what is best for you, if you are to act in your best interests rather than sabotage them, you must include thorough research as part of how you manage your life. Deep inside, you know that this is true. The tough part is remembering that fact and letting yourself follow through with this intuition, especially when your opinions appear to be fixed. But that's going to change. It starts when you STOP, listen, and research.

Research intensely and you will learn how to correct things when they go wrong. You will create a much more balanced approach to your interactions with others and to your own emotions. You will find yourself able to step back from the extremes you sometimes find yourself confronting, and you will be able to gain the perspective you need to introduce a more balanced approach to issues.

What Should You Research?

You should research the facts that you think you already know before you formulate your opinion. Defining those facts and learning to accurately distinguish fact from opinion is where you need to develop a new technique.

It's easy to become confused about exactly what you are supposed to be researching, especially if your emotions have intruded to diminish your logical capacity. In highly charged situations your emotions will prevent you from wanting to look for alternatives. There is an instinctive desire to react quickly, which represents a primal survival response.

Research exactly what is being said. Remember your listening skills (Step 2). Once again, be careful to research what was said, word for word, rather than accepting what you thought you heard. Ask questions, compare, evaluate, search. The more inquisitive you become, the better off you are. Clarify exactly what you heard to make sure you are absorbing as much information as possible. The amount of research you do and the time required to do it will vary with each situation.

Evaluate Your Research

You think you research well? Let's try it. First, read the following nursery rhyme:

> *Humpty Dumpty sat on a wall*
> *Humpty Dumpty had a a great fall*
> *All the King's horses*
> *And all the the King's men*
> *Couldn't put Humpty together again*

What did you read? Did you notice the "a a" in line two and "the the" in line four? If you didn't, what was obviously in front of you wasn't perceived by you. Why didn't you notice these words? You didn't notice them because you believed that you already knew the words that were contained in the nursery rhyme. Just because they *shouldn't* be there doesn't mean they *aren't* there.

The same lack of awareness applies to cavebrain assumptions. You may believe that you know why someone has said something to you, or you may believe that you know why you are having trouble getting through to someone else, but that doesn't necessarily mean that you actually recognized what is really getting in the way of communication. You may have missed it, but in your perceived familiarity with the person you're speaking with or your familiarity with the issue you're discussing, you may have missed what is actually there.

Now, imagine if you couldn't research the Humpty Dumpty rhyme and I insisted that there were, in fact, two a's and two the's. You would swear that they weren't there because you are convinced that you would have seen them. In this case, without the benefit of research, you would be wrong.

If you base your decisions on unresearched conclusions, you will probably keep running into the same obstacles as you usually run into, and you will not realize it. You will begin to doubt yourself and grow increasingly frustrated. Why? Because you didn't research. You didn't examine if what you believed to be true was really true.

If I were to present you with yet another item to research, chances are you would be far more alert to the details. You didn't develop any earth-shattering new skill other than a greater sense of alertness to your own tendency to assume you know exactly what's going on when, just maybe, you don't. This is the secret to research: the simple awareness of the need to do it.

LEARN THE NEW LANGUAGE OF RESEARCH

Internal research is the most fruitful research you will ever do. It will not be simple to master right away, because even though you may have used your critical faculties to examine your experiences, internal research is very much like learning a new language. When you are first learning the new language, you have to think about everything you're going to say before you say it, and you have to think about everything you hear. You take nothing for granted. You ask people to speak more slowly and you concentrate intensely on every word they say.

It's the same with Step 3. At the beginning of your research, you need to slowly and methodically gather as much information as you can about every situation that demands resolution. The surest sign that you are not researching effectively is that you reach an emotional conclusion very quickly about the situation you are in. Don't let your cavebrain fool you into thinking that you have researched when what you have done, actually, is merely dwelled on your own opinion. Take the more fruitful, but initially more time-consuming, approach: ask some questions.

Asking Questions

All research begins with inquiry. The more thoroughly you ask questions, the greater the probability that you will find out intricate facts about your situation, or facts that may not seem important at first, but prove to be critically important once you begin to consider their relevance.

Ask lots of questions. Gather as much information as possible from all relevant sources. A good question to ask yourself is: "Do I have to accept the conclusions others make when doing my research especially if I don't agree with them?" Then examine what you don't agree with and research why. The more valid your answer, the happier you will feel. If, on the other hand, you have no explanation for your feelings, the more likely it is that they are based primarily on emotions. This is your clue that more research is required.

You do not have to accept those conclusions. If you disagree with an opinion based on previous knowledge, that's fine, but always be willing to do further research if necessary.

Asking, of course, also means listening to the answers. Your listening process (Step 2) is crucial in the research phase, particularly when you hear something you don't like or when you hear something different from what you expected—*especially* when you hear something that is contrary to your own opinion.

AN OPEN MIND WILL CHANGE YOUR LIFE

One of the most surprising and puzzling things I ever heard came from South African President Nelson Mandela. It helped me re-evaluate my feelings about my own character, feelings developed during my formative years in the era of apartheid.

I was politically and socially aware of the racial injustices in my native South Africa. Nevertheless, the indoctrination of the apartheid system that discriminated against black South Africans was so strong that even though I disagreed with the policy of segregation and discrimination, I discovered as I researched my life that I held a number of remarkably inaccurate and distasteful conclusions about black South Africans.

For example, as a young man I believed that black men had no family values but simply went from one woman to another, never married, and didn't care for their children. This misconception was based on what I was taught at school, what we discussed in my peer groups, and what we heard from adults. I am ashamed at the degree to which I was indoctrinated with these beliefs. Yet I believed these "facts" unquestioningly.

The evidence appeared to confirm my negative perceptions. The woman who cleaned my home was a single mother, and one of her children, Warren, used to play with my kids. When I came home, my kids would run toward me and leap into my arms. Warren would too. I felt awkward when he did this. I told myself I felt this way because he wasn't my child. When I took the time to think about it, I asked myself: Was it because Warren wasn't my child, or because Warren was black? It bothered me tremendously that perhaps I felt awkward because of the colour of his skin. This question, and its disturbing answer, galvanized me to examine to what degree I had been instilled with racist perspectives. I began to look at things differently and change my ways.

Under apartheid, if blacks worked with you, they were not supposed to share water glasses or any utensils. It was common practice to supply black workers with their own utensils. Black employees were also actually expected to call you "master," and 99 percent did. I decided to end all these practices in my sphere of influence.

When I left South Africa in 1984, I felt that I had worked hard to ensure that I treated everyone I knew in South Africa equally, but I continued to feel guilty and ashamed that I had ever considered black people to be anything other than equals. No matter how hard I tried, all the inner research into this emotional issue yielded no resolution to my abiding sense of guilt.

Then I discovered Nelson Mandela's *The Long Road to Freedom*. In this book he describes his early days as a politically active lawyer when he was looking for financial backing and political assistance from foreign countries. He had to sneak out of the country on these trips, primarily because he didn't have a passport, and because he would never have been allowed to leave anyway. His missions were, after all, dedicated to revolutionary change in his native South Africa. It's not the sort of thing you put under "Reason for Visit."

During one trip he found himself in a Central African state, needing to be flown up to an Arab country. All was well until he discovered that the pilot of the plane was black. His immediate response was shock and worry that a black man was going to pilot the plane. He wondered how in the world a black man could know how to fly a plane. He realized that he, the most active supporter of rights and freedoms for native Africans, maintained his own preposterous prejudices towards blacks. His indoctrination, like mine, had him believing that black people were incompetent simply by virtue of the colour of their skin.

When I reached this passage in Mandela's book I was stunned. It was a liberating and sobering moment because it helped me place my own systematic indoctrination in perspective. Perhaps the struggle I was having with my own preconceptions about race did not represent, after all, an inherent flaw in my character, but rather the warped conclusions created by my education—conclusions that I could change. And I did change them.

RESEARCH YOUR EMOTION-BASED FACTS

Human beings have an insatiable need to classify and categorize experience. Sometimes you find yourself measuring what you have heard against your established set of beliefs, or information database. And the more your cavebrain attempts to protect you in highly emotional situations, the more it leaps directly into your existing information database and comes to a conclusion as quickly as possible in order to give you some manner of informed basis for action. Unfortunately, all you are doing is researching your own opinion. You are not actually researching what you have heard, which is where you really need to begin your research.

Fear makes you vulnerable to speculative and "creative" thought. Your imagination tends to fabricate all manner of facts. These facts are seldom based on reality. Indeed, the more expansive your cavebrain reactions, the more inclined you are to indulge your fears with false realities in order to justify your cavebrain's behaviour.

Why are you so inclined to indulge yourself in false realities? It's very simple: you are far more inclined not to research what you believe you know, and more inclined to research what you believe you don't know. If I ask you to go to my kitchen cupboard and tell me how many coffee mugs it contains, you will probably happily go to the cupboard and count the mugs because you have no clue how many mugs are contained there. On the other hand, if I ask you to go to your own kitchen cupboard and count your own mugs, you will probably resist doing it because of course you know that there are six coffee mugs inside, even if you haven't counted them in the last few days. Because you believe you know what the research will reveal, you don't do the research.

Until you learn to research properly, you will continue to resist change. You are perfectly willing to research anything that you feel you will learn something from, but you feel it is a waste of time to research what you believe you know, and this includes situations when you believe that your emotions are based on accurate perceptions of fact.

Unfortunately, those facts, as you know, are seldom facts when your emotions are front and centre. Emotions alter your perception, and because perceptions have no boundaries, there is no limit to irrational thought. When this happens, your sense of reality becomes plagued with imagined distortions. The very presence of these intense emotions is your signpost to conduct your research properly.

WHEN OTHERS DON'T RESEARCH

Things can go wrong very quickly when you assume facts and neglect to complete your research. I am reminded of a frustrating episode that occurred recently:

My family and I decided to take a much-needed holiday. We were looking forward to a break as we had not been away together for two years and we had gone through an intense time. This was going to be our great and glorious getaway: one week, to cram in all the relaxation and fun that we could, and we wanted nothing less than the ultimate.

Our travel agent informed us that she had done considerable research on our behalf, and recommended a holiday. It would be, she told us, the ultimate: peaceful, beautiful, and luxurious. The hotel in Mexico promised an uninterrupted ocean view, free drinks, free food, all the golf I wanted, and the most romantic setting I could imagine.

Unfortunately, the sizzle was far more enticing than the steak. In the end, the only excitement we experienced on our first night there was to listen to the incessant all-night parties. The bath in our room featured black mould sprouting from what was once presumably white sealant, and it took nearly twenty-five minutes to fill the tub, by which time the water was uninvitingly lukewarm. Moreover, the hot weather was too much for the ineffective, cacophonic air-conditioning unit. This was just as well because the heat in the room helped dry you after your bath, since the bath towels were more suited for dish towels than for drying the human body.

After the first sleepless night, I thought I might as well try the golf course. I was assured that a short ten-minute trip by cab would have me playing in no time on a championship course. It wasn't a championship course; it was a public course in horrible condition. It was a dreadful round. And then there was the beach.... The packed beach of marauding drunks and thumping dance music put me right off.

Considering we had asked for a quiet, romantic spoiled-as-you-go holiday, I was amazed at our travel agent's choice. When I queried her, she revealed that she had never been to this location; in other words, she hadn't researched this place correctly. She had based her opinions on what other people told her. She'd been told by another travel agent in her office that the hotel was unlike any other hotel in that area. That was an understatement. Can you imagine how many people had been sent to this place based on the recommendation of agents who had never been there? I'm afraid to guess.

This is what happens when people really don't research. They assume that they have researched, when all they have done is hear what they wanted to hear. This example illustrates that good research is hardly ever confined to one source. Likewise, in you attempt to research, you would be equally unwise to accept the word of any one source.

BEGIN YOUR RESEARCH WHEN EMOTIONS SWEEP YOU AWAY

Leave your research until you feel like researching and the consequences may prove disastrous—in your personal life, in your professional life, or in your financial life.

Do you recall the Bre-X investment scandal that came to light in the spring of 1997? Bre-X was the Calgary-based mining exploration company whose stocks rose from a few pennies per share to nearly $300 per share on the Toronto Stock Exchange. Then, reports were published by the company that it had discovered gold deposits in Busang, Indonesia, touted as the largest gold find in history and totalling more than 100 million ounces of readily extractable gold. After the initial announcement, Bre-X upped the estimated size of the deposit to nearly 200 million ounces.

Investors around the world were frantic with greed and glee, embarking on huge spending sprees on Bre-X stock, driving its price higher and higher and higher. The stock made a 10-1 split, making investors giddier and giddier, and they happily accepted the facts as they emerged. They rode their cavebrains' self-betterment motive onward and upward with an investment that seemed too good to be true.

There was one slight problem in this wildly exciting gold strike: no independent geological research firm had completed any drilling tests at the site to verify Bre-X's reports. Rumours began to spread that Bre-X may not have discovered the amount of gold they claimed they had. Then, shortly before the independent drilling results were published, news spread that Michael DeGuzman, the Bre-X geologist responsible for the geological data, had jumped out of, or fallen out of, a helicopter, to his death, leaving behind an eight-page suicide note. Once again, little research was done, and cavebrain panic selling began as investors attempted to protect their financial well-being. Trading of the stock was finally halted on the Toronto Stock Exchange as the computer systems recognized the pattern of trading that profiles cavebrain buying and selling.

When Toronto-based Strathcona Mineral Services finally travelled to the Busang site and completed testing, their research revealed that not only was there less than 200 million ounces of gold at the site, there was not enough gold there to bother attempting to mine in the first place. Research proved that the facts were indeed fiction. Someone—some say Michael DeGuzman—had salted the tests with gold from another location. The Bre-X fantasy, it turned out, was the greatest investment fraud perpetrated upon investors in the history of equity trading.

With the actual researched facts finally made public, Bre-X stock was allowed to trade again and people made the only intelligent investment decision left to make: sell. The price of the stock tumbled back to mere pennies. In the end, more than three billion dollars' worth of worthless stock had been issued and sold to wild-eyed individuals and investment corporations who had convinced themselves of the validity of the gold find which final research revealed to be a hoax.

Research verifies or disputes the validity of your opinions, especially when generated by your cavebrain's passions, and it gives you the power to act upon emotions based on facts.

PROMPT RESEARCH PRODUCES IMMEDIATE REWARDS

Maria is a graduate of a Witz Emotional Management System program and is an extremely talented graphic designer. She recently submitted her portfolio to a design studio, and because of the exceptional quality of her work, she was immediately offered a position at the firm.

Maria's first project was to design a brochure. She worked long into the night and came up with what she believed was her best work to date. She couldn't wait to present it to her boss. When she did, her boss said that she would look it over before presenting it to their client. Maria was confident that everyone would love it.

A few hours later Maria's boss called her in. She explained that the work was not up to the firm's standards. Maria left her boss's office devastated. Nothing was mentioned about the design or its merits. None of her design's outstanding features were even recognized. Her entire effort had been dismissed with, "It's not up to the firm's standard." Upset, Maria seriously considered quitting her job.

Fortunately, Maria used her PI. She listened to what her boss said. What do you think she should have researched at this point?

1. How unfair the criticism is?

2. The fact that her work was good enough when she presented her portfolio at her job interview, but that now suddenly everything's wrong with it?

3. The fact that her boss is a woman and most likely cannot stand the competition?

4. Opinions from other people that will at the very least highlight her design's excellent potential?

All these would be opinions and would not constitute true research. They represent the cavebrain's protective voice, saturated with opinion and emotion as it nobly attempts to protect Maria from the attack it perceives.

If Maria were to contemplate any of these thoughts, she would be reacting to what she thought was said; that is, "Your work is not good enough." But what her boss actually said was, "It's not up to the firm's standards." Is "It's not up to the firm's standards" the same as "It's not good enough?"

Can you begin to see how easy it is to hear something that has not been said? Again, the key is to research what was said, word for word, not what you thought was said. Do not research your opinions. That is just too easy to do, and the conclusions are notoriously unreliable.

Be Your Own Scientist

Understandably, when you put a lot of effort into something and you believe in your effort, it's difficult to simply accept the fact that there may be something wrong with your output.

Unfortunately, most of us react just as Maria did at first. Whether it's about a design or a report or the efforts that were made to ensure an event's success, or a personal gift, we hate criticism especially when we know how hard we tried to do a good job. It feels unfair and cruel.

But let's look at research again. In Maria's case, no research has been done. There's plenty of biased opinion. These opinions are based on non-facts. Now is the time to research. Now is the time for Maria to be her own scientist and determine if her emotions are justified or if she is following an emotional reaction that could come back to haunt her.

In Maria's situation and in most situations, a conclusion is reached almost instantaneously. You hear then you react. There is no research, only reaction.

Get Answers

How should Maria research? Take a look at her situation again. Maria must start by restricting her research to what she heard, not to what she perceived was said. Rule number one: Research only what was said. And what her boss said was, "It's not up to the firm's standards." Maria must discover what exactly makes her work not up to standard. Perhaps the design is fantastic but the presentation is not up to the firm's standards.

Maria asked her boss, "What exactly do you feel makes my design not up to standard?" She found out that her boss thought that her design was, after all, excellent, just as Maria had felt about it. The problem was with the presentation material that accompanied the design. Because she was a new employee, Maria was unaware of how the company liked to present their work: where they placed their logo, the style of presentation cover used to house the presentation, how they presented the cover letter, how many copies they made, and so on.

A few minutes of explanation clarified the facts. But without this simple research, without this one question, all kinds of disasters could have been set in motion. Quitting her job, which Maria had considered doing, would have done very little for her because, regardless of where she worked next, there would always be somebody else offering criticism of one kind or another. If she didn't learn to ask the "right" questions, Maria would end up quitting one job after another.

GIVE YOURSELF TIME TO RESEARCH

Not all research needs to take a long time. Depending on the situation and provided that you are not simply dismissing a situation, some research can be conducted in a few seconds and simply be based on tried-and-*tested* previous experience.

If at first you don't succeed try, try again. Research is not limited to a few questions. We are not accustomed to researching, especially where our emotions are concerned. So the more you practise researching, the more adept you will become.

You and only you can attest to the reliability of the source of information and the facts you gain from your research. In fact, research should initiate an internal debate. This kind of debate stimulates different points of view, and will help keep you from relying on your own opinion as your sole source of facts.

The Wrong Way to Research Is to Research Your Own Opinion

The natural tendency in research, however, doesn't produce revelation and enlightenment. Too often it leads to trouble. Take Rick's story, for example:

Rick struggled with the classic tension with his in-laws. He believed that his mother-in-law was condescending towards him. This was his opinion. Every time she said something to him, he could "feel" her criticism. He was convinced that she thought he was not good enough for her daughter, Linda. One day his mother-in-law commented on how Linda used to excel in sports before she got married. That was the final straw. Rick shouted at his mother-in-law and stormed out of the house, refusing to visit his in-laws again. Linda became just as enraged—at Rick for verbally attacking her mother, and angry at her mother for being so judgemental of her decision to marry Rick.

Rick's emotional cavebrain reaction created an interpersonal dynamic that ensured a state of increased tension and ongoing confrontation. His opinions reinforce his perceptions. He perceives that his mother-in-law does not like him, and takes whatever she says as a personal affront. While Rick's perceptions may be correct, he is not operating from a position of strength; he is merely reacting to what he perceives is a criticism. He has not researched what he listened to. He has reacted to what he thought he heard.

What if Rick's feelings of persecution had actually proved to be unfounded? What if his mother-in-law had actually been trying to share her pride in and love for her daughter? How would Rick have known without research?

If he had asked questions of his mother-in-law, perhaps he and she could have unexpectedly built an emotional bridge between them. What kind of questions could he have asked? Here are a few:

1. Why do you think Linda gave up sports?

2. Do you think that getting married interfered with her athletic ability?

3. What do you think contributed to her giving up sports?

All of these questions—provided that they are asked from a genuinely inquisitive position as opposed to an accusatory position—will reveal exactly what the speaker intended to impart. Rick may prove to be correct in his opinion that he was being blamed, in which case he could deal with that. Or his mother-in-law may simply have been reminiscing about her daughter. With Rick's unresearched reaction, only one fact emerges. Regardless of the validity of Rick's perception, the outcome is the same: a negative confrontation which reinforces Rick's negative belief.

His research very well may have revealed that his mother-in-law's comments were not directed at him as a jab but as an invitation to develop their relationship based upon the one thing they shared: their love for Linda.

Rick will never know. He hates his mother-in-law and is convinced she hates him. And she does dislike him, now that he has attacked her verbally. The doubts she may have had about him earlier have been reinforced by Rick's reaction. Rick did not research the facts. Now everyone is paying the price.

The more you practise not researching, the less you do. On the other hand, the more you practise researching, the more you will do. Practice makes perfect.

STEP 4: UPDATE YOUR OPINION— THE FACTUAL INTEGRATION OF NEW THOUGHT

After completing Steps 1, 2, and 3, you will almost certainly find that your initial emotional opinion about a situation may be outdated or out of sync with your new information.

The first three steps in the Emotional Management System—STOP, listen, research—have enabled you to review all aspects of your most emotionally charged issues. What makes this such a remarkable achievement is that you have reached this level without diminishing the importance or intensity of your emotions. The Emotional Management System has lifted you into an entirely new realm of insight and clarity that integrates powerful emotion with powerful reason.

From this new level, you now have the objectivity to examine your new feelings. As with anything, there must be a balance. You have to be sure that you avoid over-researching, which can lead to procrastination and stop you from moving forward.

YOUR OPINION IS ESSENTIAL TO EMOTIONAL MANAGEMENT

It is vital that you include your own opinions in everything you do. Therefore, you need to know how to manage them.

You need to manage these opinions because they are the rudders that steer your emotional ship. Deny your opinions or behave in a way that is inconsistent with them and you are being untrue to yourself. In this case, you will find it tremendously difficult to achieve your Position of Independence. Having carefully completed Steps 1 through 3, you will have armed yourself with the best facts available to ensure that your opinions are ultimately based on facts. Without the "real" facts, you could very well sabotage your own objectives.

The question is: What is your opinion about your situation after you have completed your research (Step 3)? Has your research confirmed your previous assumptions and strengthened your opinions, or has it shed new light on your situation so that you now have a new perspective and a new opinion?

The goal of Step 4 is to bring you to a point where you respond to your interpersonal situations with all the genuine emotion you feel. The marvel of your new system is that you now know that you can have strong opinions and be confident that they are based on sound understanding and thought, not on preconceptions. You have begun to integrate your cavebrain and your computerbrain, and you have created a synchronized, supportive approach. You are now ready to start to formulate your course of action.

WRITE DOWN YOUR OPINIONS

Always consider your situation. If you can, write down your concerns and the facts as you know and understand them. Always try to consider the facts as parts of a puzzle. Sometimes they may appear to fit where you place them, but sometimes appearances are deceiving. Be prepared to adjust their position with the emergence of new facts.

The Invalid Reason for Updating Your Opinion

Updating your opinion in order to reinforce or fuel your own emotional condition is an invalid and ineffective use of your critical faculties. In fact, in such cases you are not using your critical faculties (your computerbrain) at all. You are allowing the objectives of the cavebrain to rule. It happens all the time.

Consider Mary's father, for example. Mary approaches her parents with an idea for investing their savings. "Never!" shouts her father as he dismisses Mary's idea as "foolish and irresponsible," while her mother interjects with criticism of her own, accusing Mary of believing that it's somehow remarkably easy to accumulate money.

However, when Mary introduces the fact that her in-laws, who her parents admire and respect, have invested their savings in this scheme and have done so very successfully, Mary's father changes his mind. He expresses his new instant opinion and says, "Well, if Howard and Joan thought it was a good idea to invest, then I suppose the investment must be good."

This is a prime example of what happens when you do not trust your own opinion. Mary's parents were dead set against their daughter's idea for investing their savings before they were able to do any research. Their final decision to invest was based entirely on their opinion of Mary's in-laws' apparent financial acumen. No thought or research was devoted to evaluating whether or not investing their savings would be a wise financial move for them.

In the end they discounted their own opinion and decided to trust someone else's. This is not the computerbrain making a decision. It is the cavebrain making a decision in its usual reactive mode, substituting a feeling of fear for another equally volatile emotion: greed. Mary's parents never took responsibility for their opinion. They did not operate from a PI. So, if the investment pans out and makes them some money, they will marvel at what a wise investment decision they made; if they lose money, they will blame their daughter and her in-laws.

The Valid Reason for Updating Your Opinion

True resolution is the valid reason for updating your opinion. Invariably, the interpersonal situations which mean most to you are always destined to be the ones that require you to integrate your computerbrain capacities, and it is the computerbrain that will get you out of your cavebrain mess and into a stunning new level of interpersonal success.

Consider a situation from my family life. Some weeks ago I was walking past my teenage son's room and noticed that it was a disgusting mess. Without my emotional management system, my opinion is that if I ask him to clean up his room, he will undoubtedly argue with me and feathers will fly. With this opinion firmly in mind, I face one of two options:

1. I do not approach him because my opinion is that I "know" what the outcome will be, in which case three outcomes will occur:

   a) His room will remain a mess.

b) I will remain irritated.

c) The problem will remain with me, as will the belief that it is difficult to talk to my son on a number of issues.

or

2. I approach him, but I approach him in an aggressive manner because,
   again, my opinion is that I know he will argue with me and will not
   be willing to listen. I also assume that he will have nothing to say that
   will help resolve the situation. Not surprisingly, I do get an argument
   from him, or I shout him down. My opinion is that I am going to get
   an argument anyway, so having convinced myself of this, I may as well
   attack first. This approach usually initiates a responded-to-as-treated
   response from my son. And in the meantime, his room gets messier.

Those two approaches represent the typical polar extremes we are pulled
toward: we hope that some miracle will change the situation, or we assume
that nothing we do can improve the situation. There is no middle ground.

I consider a third option. With additional research, you find you have
the kind of meaningful content to update your opinion so that you can
move things forward. This approach enables me to loosen the grip of my
cavebrain-generated opinion, and it enables me to attempt a third option:
meaningful discussion.

I consider all the achievements my son has made in his life and I recognize that, actually, when he understands the value in something, he is
tremendously capable of applying himself. Using this internal research, I
update my opinion of his capacity to meet my expectations by discovering
a way to help him recognize a new expectation for himself.

I choose option three. I discuss the situation with my son, and tell him
how I feel about the state of his room. I convey to him the importance I
place on neatness and discipline in one's own life. I express my pride in
him and therefore my hope that he will incorporate the values of cleanli-
ness and neatness into his own life. I also discuss how unfair it is to expect
others to do the work for him, and mention my concerns for his hygiene.

Option number three is the approach that worked best for us. During
my discussion with my son I discovered that he didn't really think cleaning
up his room was important. He didn't realize to what degree the state of
his room upset me. He had never considered before how the room's disar-
ray actually said something about him, and how he placed a different value
on his achievements in public than he did on his own inner experience.

Talking to my son about cleaning up his room turned out to be a very important discussion in which each of us grew. The encounter gave my son the opportunity to find a constructive solution rather than decide beforehand that it wasn't tenable. I discovered that he was able to update his opinion on his own and was far more open to rational discussion on heated issues than I had imagined. And I discovered that I was able to move a potential confrontation into a meaningful moment of growth for both myself and my son.

My son's room isn't a science experiment anymore, and we have convinced the Department of Health that regular inspections are no longer necessary.

STEP 5: WEIGH THE PROS AND CONS— THE FREEDOM TO CONTROL THE DIRECTION YOU TAKE

You may not identify it as such, but you weigh pros and cons every day, from deciding which clothes to wear, to deciding how to prioritize your financial spending, to deciding what you are going to do on the weekend.

The trick, of course, is learning how to strategically apply this skill to emotional situations.

TAKING THE NEXT STEP

Let's review your progress so far: You have held the reins on your runaway cavebrain reactions. You have successfully integrated your computerbrain into the process. You have researched and determined the actual facts of the situation you are in—all the external facts, as well as your own gut instincts about what action you should take. Now your computerbrain can really help you. Now you gather all the information and consider the benefits or drawbacks this information presents to you.

You know that STOPPING (Step 1) is essential to giving you the opportunity to establish your Position of Independence. It also neutralizes the cavebrain long enough to enable the computerbrain to begin to integrate its input into your situation. You also know that using the first step is not a total solution. You need to use Steps 2 (Listen) and 3 (Research) to find out what's really going on. Simply learning facts and remaining stalled and passive doesn't solve a situation either. You then need to evaluate the facts, incorporate your overall goal into your plan, and take action.

With Steps 1 through 4 in place, it is time to give yourself the opportunity to finalize what you heard, what you researched, and what you concluded was your own updated opinion. It is time to introduce Step 5: weighing the pros and cons.

Let Your Computerbrain Shine

Weighing the pros and cons is an evaluative method that combines the four interrelated steps of your PI:

1. Listening to information

2. Gathering information

3. Researching information

4. Augmenting information by introducing your own updated opinion

Think of this stage as a self-checking process. Once you have all the information at your disposal, you can add it all together. This is the place within your Position of Independence that allows you to think through all the issues that you are facing. You will now find that an updated opinion has emerged. It is a wonderful step because at this point, your thinking will be far clearer and more precise, and it will be based on careful consideration, not emotional reaction.

MOVING FROM DECISION MAKING TO ACTION TAKING

Steps 1 through 4 have given you the tools you need to integrate the computerbrain with your cavebrain during the review stage of any situation. You have now re-established an integrated platform for effective decision making. Now it is necessary to protect this platform as you move from making a balanced decision to taking effective action. Regardless of the integrated thinking you achieved in Steps 1 through 4, the prospect of taking action can often derail the integrated cavebrain-computerbrain thinking you have achieved so far.

It is all too easy to go through all the steps in the Emotional Management System and arrive at an objective which quickly becomes misdirected or corrupted. This happens when you substitute an emotional approach to your overall objective. You lose control of the balanced integrated objective that meets the needs of both your emotions and your rational thinking. The process of weighing the pros and cons enables you to take a different direction to the one dictated by your cavebrain.

So how can you control the direction you take? You do this by ensuring that your objective is based on positive, not negative, intentions. To understand this, let us first look at an objective in simple terms: an objective is a desire to achieve an end result.

OBJECTIVE = DESIRE

Between desire and result is the all-important link: method. A quick reflective computerbrain moment here can determine whether or not the method you intend to use is compatible with the end result or if the method corrupts it.

Consider this example: A sales manager has been contacted by corporate headquarters and pressured to increase sales volumes in his region to the level of other similarly sized regions. He then wants to get the message out to his sales team: more effective effort is needed so they can achieve higher sales. He assembles his team and, afraid of missing his sales goals (note cavebrain emerging), he decides that unless he resorts to threats, he will not achieve his ultimate goal. Consequently, he threatens to fire each member of the sales team if they don't boost sales by 15 percent within 8 weeks.

Let's review the sales manager's objective: increased sales. Is the resulting method going to negatively or positively influence his objective? Answer: It is going to negatively affect his objective. The goal he actually achieves is a threatened sales team. A threatened sales team is a fearful and demoralized one (note cavebrain response), and cavebrain reactions are unlikely to maintain the goodwill and energy necessary to fulfill the intended objective.

The purpose of weighing the pros and cons is to consider all the facts and to ensure that your cavebrain opinion does not hijack the decision-making process. The sales manager was unable to separate his fear from his course of action. His fearful, cavebrain-centred method is incompatible with the objective he hopes to achieve. Ironically, his approach will likely lead to even lower sales. What he needed to do was to determine if his method negatively or positively supports his objective. Would a cavebrain approach positively support a computerbrain objective?

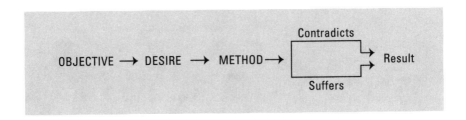

Weighing the pros and cons allows you to contemplate all the factors you need to consider before attempting to reach an objective. Consider the sales team example once more, but now apply a method to the situation that will positively support the objective: a factual review of the situation with his staff. The method he uses to tell his sales team about the need to increase sales is as follows: he identifies the details of the situation, asks for input, researches options and new approaches, shares information, develops and expresses potential—good or bad—and motivates his team to press on. This approach does not corrupt the end result. The result is positively charged as it looks for resolution and avoids emotional confrontation.

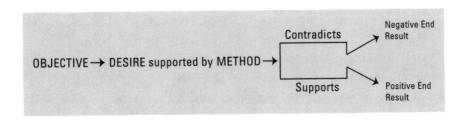

Chapter 18

BALANCED MIND, BALANCED ACTION

If the computerbrain is integrating with the cavebrain's input, you will be able to look at your objective and method and determine whether they are compatible. However, if the cavebrain is dominating the consideration process, establishing emotional boundaries in any emotional, confrontational, or negative situation becomes your primary objective. You are always ready for opposition to your intended objective. The positive objective becomes lost in cavebrain-dominated reactions. When this happens, you become predisposed to being accusatory, confrontational, and intimidating from the start.

How well does the negative approach work? Not very well. People are less than enthusiastic about supplying confrontational people with what they are requesting. The positive result you want can be sabotaged because the cavebrain dictates that expressing your emotion about a situation is more important than achieving the resolution you want. Always ask yourself: Is the method compatible with the objective?

What do you do next? Allow yourself to recognize if your objective could potentially become a cavebrain trigger. Then use your computerbrain by projecting how your cavebrain-dominated objective will play out in the end. Generally, if you are focused, you will realize that such a negative approach will create a new dynamic even further removed than ever from your objective. This is the process of weighing the pros and cons.

Step 4 is seldom mastered the first time you try it. The whole idea of weighing the pros and cons is to prevent the negatively charged expectations from polluting your decisions. So, if you have reached Step 4 and you still find yourself favouring a negatively charged objective to one that is positively charged, then recall Step 1: STOP. STOP and consider the situation. Recognize that it doesn't make sense to allow the method of approach to corrupt your desired result, and bring yourself back on track.

Remember that the STOP concept is not an isolated, one-time-only step. STOPPING is the neurophysical trigger or tool you use to return to a balanced position of integrated cavebrain-computerbrain thinking at any time and during any step in the Emotional Management System.

You cannot integrate and use the important data you gained while listening, researching, and updating your opinion if your method corrupts the result you are trying to achieve. Weighing the pros and cons is a process that allows you to get the balanced, natural flow of thought and action to return to rational decision making. Step 4 in the Emotional Management System helps to release you from your cavebrain's agenda so that you can freely determine a course of action that is in the best interests of you and everyone around you.

Weighing the pros and cons gives you options. And when you have options, you have freedom.

WEIGHING SECURITY AGAINST INSECURITY

Now let's put the process of weighing the pros and cons to work. In my years of working with people, I have found that affairs of the heart are certainly the most difficult to manage effectively. Consider the following scenario:

Suzanne has been going out with Michael for the past sixteen months. Everything was fine until Michael's ex-girlfriend, Rachel, reappeared on the scene. Despite Michael's constant reassurances that Rachel meant nothing to him, Suzanne reacted emotionally. She felt angry and suspicious. Her suspicion and anger increased when she found out that Rachel was calling Michael at work.

The situation took a turn for the worse when Michael, who was comfortable enough to be completely honest, told Suzanne that he was going to meet Rachel for coffee in an attempt to persuade her to leave him alone. The only relationship he was interested in was with Suzanne. Suzanne, however, could not understand why Michael found it necessary to have a meeting with his ex-girlfriend. Her insecurity bred more insecurity. She felt threatened, and this is when the cavebrain performs at its most efficient level.

EVALUATING YOUR CHOICES

If you were Suzanne and found yourself in a similar situation, which option would you follow? What are the pros and cons of each option?

Option A

Forbid Michael from having any contact with his ex-girlfriend.

PRO You would eliminate the rendezvous and thus also eliminate the specific potential consequences of the meeting.

CON Michael would feel you are trying to control his life and he would resent the ultimatum, thus giving you a potentially more volatile problem to deal with. This is a cavebrain solution.

Option B

Threaten Michael with ending the relationship if he insists on meeting with Rachel.

PRO You stand up for yourself and leave the fate of the relationship in Michael's hands.

CON You risk losing your relationship over what may have proven to be a non-issue. Or worse, your intolerant ultimatum may, in the end, repel Michael so much that you drive him away from you. This is a cavebrain solution.

Option C

Tell Michael that if he really loved you and really cared about and respected your feelings, he wouldn't meet with Rachel.

PRO You are expressing your feelings and you hope this will sway Michael.

CON You prove that you are the one who obviously doesn't respect his feelings, which include his dedication to your relationship, and you risk distancing yourself from him further. This is a cavebrain solution.

Option D

Insist that you go with Michael to the meeting.

PRO You would be able to monitor the meeting, intimidate both Michael and his ex-girlfriend, and prevent any natural closeness from occurring between the two.

CON You would prevent the caring closeness Michael might need in order to make the situation clear to his ex-girlfriend, thus leaving Michael wondering why you don't trust him. And if you don't trust him, he will wonder if you really love him or only need him. If Michael is more interested in being loved than needed, your relationship is probably headed for the rocks. This is a cavebrain solution.

Option E

Trust Michael and/or your relationship enough even though this meeting bothers you. Express your concerns but reinforce your belief in the relationship. You might say, "I would be lying if I said I was happy about you meeting Rachel." You could also ask Michael if he felt that meeting with his ex-girlfriend is the only way to solve the issue. You could ask Michael if he would like your input. It would be necessary to reinforce his decision if he was adamant that meeting Rachel was the right approach.

PRO You show confidence in both Michael and the relationship you share. Expressing your feelings from the computerbrain is a very liberating experience.

CON You have no control over the rendezvous or anything that happens after it.

At first glance none of the above options would put Suzanne at ease, so which one would you choose?

If you chose A, B, C, or D, your relationship will most likely not advance and the situation you find yourself in will likely become more troubled and precarious. You need an approach that integrates your cavebrain's protective reactions with your computerbrain's rationality. Option E, especially if you're insecure, does not appear to be great either.

However, if your self-esteem is intact, Option E is the only option that will provide you with a platform for rational thought and therefore a rational approach to the situation. And it is the only option that treats your relationship as a healthy relationship. You make a decision from a position of strength rather than weakness. The outcome is much more likely to satisfy you. Think about it for a moment. If your partner is going to be dishonest with you, then you do not have a strong relationship to begin with. The only satisfaction that can be gained is the very short-term benefit of venting your frustration. And if your relationship continues, your experience will be merely a series of frustrated emotional outbursts. Not a very enticing prospect.

WEIGHING ACTION AGAINST INACTION

Here's another example of weighing pros and cons: Eugene had worked for IBM for fifteen years and was very good at his job. Then the recession struck and rumours were rampant that for the first time in the company's history IBM would downsize. Jobs would be on the line. What options did Eugene have, given his current objective: to survive, to maintain his standard of living, to establish a long-term solution?

Option A

Eugene did not panic although he was angry. He STOPPED. He listened to and researched the facts.

Fact 1   There is a recession.

Fact 2   People throughout the industry are being laid off.

Fact 3   He feels extremely insecure.

Fact 4   He concludes that it is unlikely that he would be able to obtain another position because of his age.

Based on these facts, Eugene decides to sit tight and do nothing in the hope that the rumours are not true so nothing will change. This is a cave-brain solution.

Option B

Eugene looked at the facts as he perceived them.

Fact 1   He has been working for IBM for fifteen years.

Fact 2   He is very good at his job.

Fact 3   IBM is the company that, up until now, has employed people for life.

Fact 4   There is a possibility that he might lose his job. Eugene is angry. He decides that rather than see if the rumours are true and wait to be retrenched, he will quit and find another job. This is a cavebrain solution.

Option C

Eugene looks at the situation. It does not look particularly promising. He decides to explore his options. He starts by investigating what his retirement package would be if he was to leave. He researches outside job prospects. He considers the worst-case scenario. He begins to make plans. He proceeds one step at a time.

Which option would you choose? Remember, you are not personally or emotionally involved and therefore it is easier for you to approach the situation logically. The dispassionate way you are able to process the information in Eugene's situation is exactly the state that Eugene needs to cultivate.

The cavebrain has prompted Eugene to act. Now he needs to balance that fevered state with the analytical and solution-oriented capacity of the computerbrain. This is why it is important to STOP first and begin the process of listening and researching. After all, it is extremely difficult to keep the emotional fever high when your approach begins to become so logical.

INSIDE EUGENE'S THOUGHT PROCESSES

If you are Eugene and you chose either Option A or Option B, you would be accepting the "facts" without the benefit of question or analysis. This acceptance would not be in your best interests.

Option A is the ostrich approach. You bury your head and do nothing in the hope that nothing further will happen and the problem will vanish.

But bad situations have a tendency to get worse, not better. Inaction merely generates a mental burden and further suffering that often triggers the tendency to not make any decision at all.

In Option A, Eugene refuses to deal with the reality of the situation. If his worst fears are realized, he will be ill prepared to deal with them and even less prepared to follow an alternative strategy. When he attempts to rectify his position, Eugene will be doing so from a weakened position.

Option B, quitting, is a pure gamble. Eugene might find a better job; he might not. The decision to leave is based on a combination of anger and fear—a combination that makes emotions the central decision-making factor in place of integrating emotion and rational thought. Little long-term good can come from basing a decision on this state of emotional upheaval. This is why regardless of the stimuli you are presented with, your process of interpretation must always follow a balanced process arising from a Position of Independence.

Option C gives Eugene a rational approach. This option will work because it integrates the cavebrain's worry, care, and concern with the computerbrain's determination to reach a self-supporting solution.

Eugene considers all his options and alternatives. He researches, formulates a plan, and proceeds in an organized way. His approach to the situation is precise and planned. Once Eugene managed to integrate his thinking with his emotionally driven speculations, he was able to make a plan. Ultimately, Eugene accepted a substantial severance package and used the lump sum to start his own business.

THE DAWN OF FREEDOM

Perhaps after reading Eugene's story, you might argue that there is little or no time to indulge in this reflective, analytical thought when you are confronted with emotionally charged issues. You may say that actions speak louder than thoughts and words. You may further argue that if you take the time to integrate your computerbrain's input into your decision making, you may lose out in some way. You won't.

Think for a moment: How many times have you made a comment in the heat of the moment that you wish you could take back if you had a second chance? And for each of those regretted moments, don't you wish you had given more consideration to the ramifications of your actions? And don't you wish that you had thought things through a little more so that you could have acted in a way that helped your life in the long term rather than satisfying your cavebrain reactions in the short term? Practise Step 5. Weigh the pros and cons before making a decision and taking action. This approach will take you one step farther from the tyranny of the cavebrain. Unless you're in mortal danger, a step farther is always the right decision to make.

19

STEP 6: DEFINE YOUR OBJECTIVE— THE WISDOM TO RECOGNIZE THE DESTINATION

The Emotional Management System puts you in control of emotional situations you never dreamed were manageable. In the previous chapter, both Suzanne and Eugene have effectively weighed the pros and cons of their situations. In both scenarios, a number of options were available to each of them, but, other than emotion, there was no guiding principle with which to determine the options that they should take.

Isn't this frequently the case with you, too?

You find yourself in a situation, you process the situation enough to generate not only a single action you could take, but a number of possible actions. You weigh each one. They all seem able to achieve one thing or another. What is missing, however, is a defined objective. Define your objective and you will always be able to select the action option that will work for you. It's like driving a car. You have a vehicle, gas, reliable brakes, and you know how to drive, but without a fixed destination, the trip would take on a life of its own, with you likely ending up where you don't want to go.

TRUST YOURSELF IMPLICITLY

In mastering Steps 1 through 5, you have given yourself the opportunity to examine yourself, your opinions, and your emotional reactions. You have questioned and you have applied a healthy dose of self-scepticism— all in order to see yourself and your situation clearly. You are balancing your emotions. You are balancing the influence of your cavebrain with your computerbrain.

By the time you reach Step 6 you see yourself and your situation more clearly than ever. You have achieved a balanced, integrated view. Now you can form a clear idea of what your situation is and how you wish it would change.

After all the work you have done, you have earned the right to consider your own objectives and goals and what is sound and in your best interests. You have the right to make your own decisions, free from the restrictions of emotions and outside approval, but balanced with responsibility. You have been totally responsible, not only towards yourself but also towards those around you. There is no feeling in the world like knowing you have prepared yourself to make the best decision you could ever make right at this very moment. This is trust—complete trust—in yourself. It is a true PI.

This feeling is so powerful because it enables you to make a decision you can live with. This is freedom, and freedom is the blessing we all need, just when we need it most.

THE OBJECTIVE BECOMES CLEAR

My father was struck by a car in 1991. He died a few months later at the age of 83. Surprisingly, he didn't die from his injuries, but from cancer, which no one knew he had been battling.

His health deteriorated steadily until finally he was admitted to hospital. Doctors discovered his disease and the advanced stage to which it had progressed. They told us that, in effect, there was no point in keeping him in the hospital, and that we must take him home. I suddenly found myself faced not only with a dying father, but also with a mother gripped by panic. She was devastated, feeling that she could not handle my father's needs in their apartment.

We learned about an agency known as Hospice, a facility where terminally ill people are given compassionate care before they die. The hospice responded immediately to my call. A nurse there recommended that I see a counsellor. I, of course—a professional who has made his living helping people deal with every emotional stress imaginable—tried to decline. After further gentle coaxing from the nurse, however, I agreed. I met with a caring woman who encouraged me to help my father to let go.

I listened to her calmly. I asked her and the attending physicians many questions about my father's pain and the morphine he was being treated with, and their prognosis, and everything I could possibly think of to help me appreciate what my father was going through. I finally understood (even though I did not accept it easily) that my father really was dying and that the counsellor was right: if he could accept his coming death too, then perhaps he could pass through life's greatest transition as peacefully and painlessly as possible.

Here I was, wanting my father to live, and on the other hand being asked to, in effect, encourage him to die sooner than his body might have been ready to. I weighed the pros and cons of the dilemma again and again.

A couple of mornings later, I woke up and realized that I wanted my father to die in an atmosphere of love and joyfulness. And if helping him avoid the terrible pain and anguish of hanging on to a few more weeks or months would enable him to die on his own terms, then I would do everything I could to help him make peace with his mortality and leave us and this world with strength and dignity.

My objective was clear. And so I spoke with my father and spent meaningful time with him as he accepted that his life was at an end. He accepted his own mortality with grace. He died in peace not long afterward, and I miss him.

DEFINING YOUR OBJECTIVE

Not all objectives are life-or-death decisions but they often feel that way. Whatever your situation, define a clear objective for yourself. Whatever decision you have to make, whatever action you have to take, it will be a decision based on more than just emotion. Mistakes will be made, but at least you took action and responsibility. This state of moving forward can be evaluated and re-evaluated so that you can meet each challenge in a balanced and healthy way until its resolution. This is the power of the Emotional Management System. This is how you will change your life.

Every mistake leads to the search for a solution. Such is the nature of humankind. When you are fearful of mistakes, you remain trapped in your situation. Fear and insecurity breeds dependency. Self-reliance and self-respect produce your Position of Independence.

STEP 7: GO—THE ALIGNMENT IS COMPLETE

When you're ready to go, you go—whether you go to work, to the movies, to the store, on a date, or for a walk. Often, though, you go whether you feel you are prepared to or not. You now have the tools to prepare yourself to go forward with a course of action that will be in your best interests and in the best interests of those around you.

When you reach Step 7 of the Emotional Management System, you have successfully created the bridge between your cavebrain and your computerbrain that enables you to manage emotional moments with emotional intelligence.

This integration of cavebrain with computerbrain is a balanced state of high emotional intelligence. It is your Position of Independence. Sometimes you will establish your PI relatively quickly. Other times it may take hours, days, even weeks. There is no deadline for reaching a PI. The only action you need to take now is to engage the course of action you have chosen in Step 6 (Define your objective), then enjoy the freedom of living your life from your strong Position of Independence.

WIN THE BATTLE OF INERTIA

Inertia is the main challenge you face when engaging any course of action that will achieve your objective. You experience inertia frequently in your life. For example, you have a tooth that is suddenly cold sensitive. You are terrified of the dentist's drill, so you don't go for a checkup. How often have you heard someone with a toothache say, "I don't have time to go to the dentist." But what happens if there is a problem? It usually gets worse. By not taking action, your situation can only get worse.

Consider this: non-action is still an action; a non-action is still a choice. By deciding not to do anything, you are doing something, which in this case is nothing—leaving the situation alone to direct its own course. It is a decision. You never want to be in a position where situations manage you. You want to manage your situations.

No situation remains the same. It either gets better or worse. The remarkable benefit of going through the Emotional Management System is that each step leads you progressively through your fears and anxieties and helps you move ahead with decisions and actions founded in logic and reason. You will feel like new. And the new you will always still be you.

Apply Your System Now and Watch Your Life Change

How long does it take to apply the Emotional Management System? How long does it take to turn a powerful emotional reaction into a meaningful self-supporting choice?

As you begin to practise your emotional management system, you will get better and better at it and you will apply the steps faster and faster. You will be able to apply the system to some challenges in a matter of seconds or minutes; other challenges may take days or weeks. For example, avoiding road rage and managing your reaction to a driver who cut you off can take a matter of seconds as you process the steps quickly. On the other hand, if you lose your job or if a romantic relationship ends or if someone you love dies, it may take you longer to meet the emotional challenge, but you will be able to manage your life far better than before because you have a system.

Many people never successfully handle the emotions that arise in such events. But you will. The Emotional Management System will let you lead yourself into a Position of Independence that enables you to give yourself permission to feel the pain you will naturally feel, but will then give you the power to manage that pain and integrate it into the meaning of your life.

When you are approaching exciting new opportunities, with their attendant triumphs and tragedies, your Position of Independence will help you remain balanced and focused as you perform at the peak of your emotional and intellectual capacities.

Make Mistakes But Learn More
from Each One

We are often terrified of making mistakes. That is unfortunate because you learn more from mistakes than from any other experiences. Mistakes are pivotal points that reveal opportunity.

When you make a mistake you have two alternatives: you can develop an avoidance response and try to remove yourself completely from the consequences of your error; or you can learn from your mistake, use it as part of your research and engage in positive remedial action.

The Position of Independence you achieve by applying your emotional management system will not prevent you from making mistakes, but it will help you drastically reduce the number of mistakes you make as a result of your cavebrain's runaway emotional momentum.

With your strong PI you will approach all situations in a structured, balanced way that integrates your feeling with your thinking, producing a response that will take you to a satisfying new level of accomplishment.

CHALLENGE YOURSELF

Outline a situation in which you can illustrate the Position of Independence principle. In forty words or less, describe your situation.

Example 1

My manager has treated me in a critical and demanding manner. I believe that he has not taken the facts into consideration. I am unable to deal with him as he is very abrupt and aggressive, besides I don't have to be treated this way!

or:

I have a staff member who neglected to ensure that the promotional material arrived on time. She simply does not listen to what I am saying. I should not have to run after her but it seems that if I don't, the work doesn't get done! This is not the first time such an incident has occurred and I believe that unless I deal with this matter firmly, I will end up doing the work for her. This will set a bad example.

Now that you have looked at some examples of other people, test an example of your own.

List the seven steps of the Emotional Management System:

1. _____

(hint: you start by . . .)

2. _____

(hint: you can't deal with something you haven't heard.)

3. _____

(hint: if in doubt, ask.)

4. _____

(hint: everyone loves this one.)

5. _____

(hint: sift the wheat from the chaff.)

6. _____

(hint: without this, what is there to talk about?)

7. _____

(hint: nothing's stopping you now.)

USING THE EMOTIONAL MANAGEMENT SYSTEM TO RESOLVE SITUATIONS

Example: "I am being treated unfairly."

Before I react, let me STOP. What am I STOPPING? I am STOP-PING the flood of emotions based only on my own perception of the situation.

Having STOPPED, I need to understand what is going on, so the second step is to LISTEN. But listen to what? Am I listening to myself (my own opinion) or am I listening to myself describe the situation?

Describe the situation—it is a good idea to write it down.

Now, to ensure that I am not merely intensifying my own opinions, I need to RESEARCH. I need to ask myself some questions: How do I feel right now? Answer: angry. What exactly has happened? I've been shouted at. What action on my part caused this reaction? Let me ask for some outside opinions on my situation (be mindful to give facts, not opinions).

Having considered everything you have revealed so far, you can ask: What do I want to do about it? I know I want to deal with the situation and I will define my true objective in the appropriate place.

Have I considered all the contributing factors? List the factors that contribute to my being angry. List the factors that may have contributed to my treatment. (I must avoid bringing in my own opinion at this stage.) Having completed my list, let me now UPDATE MY OPINION. I believe that I made an error, but the shouting was unfair and I was treated badly. (I must be careful not to allow this to override my entire Position of Independence.) However, I accept the principle that there is no substitute for taking responsibility.

Let me now reflect upon all that I have done so far and WEIGH THE PROS AND CONS. I consider all that took place—the event, my feelings, the subsequent action that led me to this point. Do I proceed or let it go?

Now I am fully prepared to formulate the action I wish to take, so I DEFINE MY OBJECTIVE. My objective becomes clear. I am going to approach my boss, reveal my concerns, and accept responsibility for the error, but in the event that I make future errors, I want to be treated with respect. There is only one thing left to do: GO and carry out my objective.

Now go through your situation as illustrated in the example on page 209.

Through this procedure, you have achieved control over how you manage your emotions and reactions. You have aligned your cavebrain reactions and your computerbrain objectivity in order to make the connection that allows you to approach interactions appropriately and effectively. In the process, you have helped build your self-esteem. Moreover, you are being proactive, not reactive.

Journal Entry

*A mistake is worth
a thousand
non-events.*

PART IV

APPLYING THE EMOTIONAL MANAGEMENT SYSTEM

21

KICK-STARTING THE EMOTIONAL MANAGEMENT SYSTEM

What follows are the stories of two individuals who learned the Emotional Management System during training sessions at the Witz Training facilities.

WHAT'S MINE IS MINE

In the following example, John is confronted not only by his own predispositions but also by another person's perceptions and predispositions and emotional reactions.

John's story:

> I have always considered myself to be reasonable and fair. I am considerate of others and most people find me easygoing. I am married to a wonderful person. Her name is Pamella. We have been married six years. We have no children. There will be plenty of time for that.
>
> Pam enjoys a variety of movies and consequently will want to go and see any garbage. I am more selective. I figure that why go and see a bad movie when there are so many good ones showing. Recently, I butted heads with her over our differences.

Pam: Hey, John, this movie looks good. It's a romantic comedy with Julia Roberts, she's fabulous. Let's go and see it. It's showing at the mall,
John: I don't want to see that garbage.
Pam: How can you say it's garbage? I've heard great things about it. The trailer looks really good and the critics liked it.

John: They don't know what they're talking about.
Pam: But John, I really want to see the movie.
John: No. It's a waste of time.
Pam: You know, John, I go with you to all those guy movies you want to see. Sometimes it would be nice if we went to see something that I want to see.
John: Arghgh.
Pam: Fine, then I'll go and see the movie on my own.
John: If you want to, go right ahead.
Pam: Geez, John, I try so hard with you, but you're so incredibly selfish. You only think of yourself. All we ever end up doing is what you want to do all the time. I'm sick of it. And you know what? I don't even know why we are married.

John was locked in his own opinion without really listening to Pam or researching what she was saying to see if what she was saying might actually be valid. He was locked in cavebrain.

Pam, on the other hand, through her overly tolerant disposition, has allowed the situation to reach a point of breakdown which could escalate to crisis proportions. The emotions that have been triggered are no longer confined to the immediate issue: which movie to see. The situation has become a catalyst for her to bring up a cocktail of frustrations that have accumulated to the point where she is openly questioning the strength and validity of the marriage itself.

Both John and Pam are displaying extremely typical positions of cavebrain domination. They are in cavebrain mode, protecting the survival of their emotional positions. Because they have not integrated their cavebrain and computerbrain functioning, they are not considering their individual and unified best interests. To that moment, the last thing on either of their minds is the realization of what is happening, and ultimately what they are doing to each other. If they continue interacting this way, they will more than likely become another divorce statistic.

John's story continues:

> I thought about the Emotional Management System I was learning. Yes, it was to try to aid my cause at work, but it kind of dawned on me that I was in the same kind of interpersonal mess at home as I was at work. I decided to give the Emotional Management System a try in this situation with Pam. I applied Step 1: the STOP concept, and this is what happened.

Pam: Geez, John, I try so hard with you, but you're so incredibly selfish. You only think of yourself. We end up doing what you want to do all the time. I'm sick of it. And you know what? I don't even know why we are married.

John (thinking): At the time, I knew I had to STOP. I wasn't listening to Pam anymore. I was becoming annoyed. I saw myself as the fair-minded, considerate individual. At this point I had no reason to change my mind. But then, why was I being faced with such an intense barrage of accusations? Was our relationship really heading for major meltdown?

> I was quiet for a moment. And I began to realize that my interactions with Pam had subtly deteriorated since we had first gotten together. I found myself confronted with these cavebrain emotional outbursts on an ever-increasing basis. It was easy to blame Pam for what was going wrong, but I think it was because I really cared and was afraid of losing her that I knew I had to use the techniques of the Emotional Management System I had recently learned. What I was currently doing certainly wasn't helping me.

John (still thinking): STOP, John, just STOP. But STOP what? STOP everything. My mind is racing. I must STOP before I can begin listening (Step 2). I must want to listen to what she's saying even though right now I feel like I disagree.
Pam: If you actually cared about me, you would...
John: Pam, do you really feel that way?
Pam: Well, John, how on earth do you expect me to feel?
John (thinking): Try and STOP, John. Don't hook yourself. STOP. Okay. Okay. Now listen to what she is saying.
John: How often am I actually like this?

The reality is that John doesn't like criticism, and his behaviour and mannerisms leave much to be desired. His decision to try to use what he had learned was attributed more to Pam's reaction than to his understanding of the situation and how to improve it.

This unfortunately is the reality of life. Human beings take so much for granted. It always saddens me to observe that we do very little to help ourselves to prevent these unnecessary problems from occurring. However, what is even sadder is our propensity to resist change and remain transfixed by the "facts" as we perceive them through our cavebrain's preformed filter of opinion, instead of following the emotionally intelligent option of allowing the computerbrain to play an active role in identifying the validity of the facts as accurately as possible. It is at that point that we become soberly aware of the genuine facts of a situation, whether we are pleased about those facts or not. And then we can resolve issues effectively.

It is awareness that is the key to change for John. The Emotional Management System allows him to achieve that awareness.

John has STOPPED again. He is listening because he has to. I wish I could say it is because he wants to, but at least he is listening. With his question to Pam—"How often am I actually like this?"—he has started to research. If he recognizes that he is researching and genuinely asks questions for which he is seeking information, and if he uses the information within all of the prescribed seven steps, then he is working from a Position of Independence, liberated from the domination of the cavebrain.

Later, John explained:

> Because of years of disqualifying her needs, it took some persuading to get Pam to accept my sincerity about looking at issues in this new way. At first it was really awkward for me to use the Emotional Management System. I would just get so reactive every time one of those "issues" got raised in my interactions with Pam. And sometimes I never even remembered the Emotional Management System when we would get into one of our head-butting sessions.
>
> But I was able to remember to apply the Emotional Management System more and more often, mostly because when I did manage to use it, things went a lot better between us. Eventually the combination of STOPPING, listening and researching enabled me to begin interacting with Pam as opposed to "knowing" how she felt, and "knowing" what I thought I knew.

The hardest part of the Emotional Management System process is dealing with one's own opinion. It must be dealt with cautiously. John's own opinion was, after all, a major contributor to the problem that he and Pam were facing.

John was able to STOP reacting purely from his own opinion. He started to listen and research. He began to consider his own opinions in a balanced and unbiased manner and as part of the process but not as the entire process. Then he was able to weigh the pros and the cons of maintaining the status quo or acting on the information generated by the Emotional Management System. He defined his objective, which was to do what he had to do to try to fix what was wrong with the relationship and move his relationship with Pam to a deeper level of connection.

John continues:

> Pam was pretty surprised by it all.
>
> Not only did using the Emotional Management System help us resolve some little issues, it set up a kind of new level of caring between us. The things that were different about us as individuals stopped always being a source of confrontation. Instead, we started to respect our differences more and we began to see that we didn't have to have the same views on everything to be in harmony with each other.

It is said that hindsight is twenty-twenty. It is easy to look back on a situation and consider what you would have done differently. The Emotional Management System is the tool you can use to plan each step with forethought, discipline, and purpose. With each success, you strengthen your belief in yourself and your ability. You change the "I wish I had" position to an "I did it right" position.

You are positively strengthening and enhancing your position by not facilitating an undesired spontaneous reaction. Rather, you are giving yourself an opportunity for alternative decision and action.

MIRROR, MIRROR

In this second example, Karin is confronted by the tremendous force of a preformed opinion and the fallout from the consequent cavebrain reactions her opinions create.

Karin's story:

> I discovered that the most beneficial use for my Position of Independence was between myself and me. That may almost sound silly, but I was truly my own worst enemy.
>
> Looking back at it all now I am amazed at how negative I was about everything. When things go wrong, it's funny how easily you slip into a negative mode. I was in a rut. I hated my job, I hated my life, and the more everyone told me how fortunate I was and how lucky I was, the more miserable I felt.

I discovered a great way to apply my emotional management system was through diary entries. It allowed me to focus on my needs from a somewhat detached perspective. These were some of the relevant entries.

ENTRY: FRIDAY, FEBRUARY 10

As I sit writing in my diary I have a feeling of great fear. I'm feeling very isolated and very disconnected. I've recently recognized my need for a permanent relationship and it seems to have reached a level of urgency. However, the energy involved in going out there on the market seems enormous and completely overwhelming. I seem to be contradicting myself, but even with all the urgency I'm feeling, there is also an incredible feeling of lethargy. How can all these emotions take place at the same time?

ENTRY: SUNDAY, FEBRUARY 12

I have just come back from a long drive north into cottage country. I travelled for miles and miles, aimlessly. The drive seemed to reflect my life. I feel like I am going nowhere. My confusion intensifies my real pain. I am going nowhere. I really am.

What is it I am not seeing? Or is it that I don't want to look at it? I'm going to have to think about that for a while.

ENTRY: SUNDAY, FEBRUARY 12, MUCH LATER

After some consideration, I realize that I must try to approach this in some way that actually lets me get going. I've got to be more logical about this thing if I can. I need a logical starting point, so I'm going to try the Emotional Management System. What better starting point is there than STOPPING.

I must STOP. I am going to STOP writing and focus on emptying my mind of all thoughts.

I like to think of Step 1: STOPPING, as the easiest of the hardest steps to do. And as I always say to people who come to learn the Emotional Management System, please don't underestimate how difficult it is to STOP. And when you find it hard to do, don't get too frustrated, because as far as I'm concerned, even thinking about STOPPING is a big step. It's like a mini step of the first step. It will come, and it will come faster than you think. Like any discipline, with repetition it becomes a habit. The decision to STOP is made by you. Once you are able to STOP, you've begun a logical process. Applying the steps enables you to establish the best emotional intelligence pattern you can achieve. You reach a Position of Independence and you can approach situations with focus and energy.

Karin's entry continued:

I feel blank right now. I am going to start by reading my previous entry.

As I sit writing in my diary I have a feeling of great fear. I'm feeling very isolated and very disconnected. I've recently recognized my need for a permanent relationship and it seems to have reached a level of urgency. However, the energy involved in going out there on the market seems enormous and completely overwhelming. I seem to be contradicting myself, but even with all the urgency I'm feeling, there is also an incredible feeling of lethargy. How can all these emotions take place at the same time?

> I must listen to what I am saying. Okay, so what's my objective? No, wait...don't rush it. Listen to exactly what you are saying first.

You have probably noted by now exactly where Karin is in the Emotional Management System. She is at Step 1. She has STOPPED. And with her last statement she is receptive to listening. Once Karin is able to listen, you will see how easily she begins to research.

> Karin (thinking): I'm saying that I have great fear, I feel isolated, I feel lethargic and there is urgency. Okay, Karin, first question: Fear of what? Answer: Fear of being alone. Question: How long have you been alone? Answer: Too long! That's the whole problem. No, now try to stick to the question. Okay, again, fear of what? Fear of failure and fear of rejection. Would that lethargy of mine have something to do with this? Am I being protective of myself and using lethargy as an excuse? So what am I actually afraid of? Fear of rejection. What do I want? I want a relationship. Stop again, Karin. Are you not jumping to objective again? Work this one through.
>
> If I want a relationship, do I not need to broaden my social activities? What have I got so far? The lethargy is an excuse. I have approached this too narrowly. But hey, I am entitled to my fear. If I wasn't afraid, I wouldn't have the desire to make anything change, after all.

Karin has weighed the pros and cons. She has spent a long time dealing with this issue. She is moving from strength to strength. Now that she has begun the process and accepted responsibility for her actions and thoughts, Karin has come to the conclusion that she can indeed change. Only now is she able to define a course of action. She has successfully launched the

Emotional Management System. The difference is that she arrives at her objective through a more emotionally intelligent perspective, defined from an integrated cavebrain–computerbrain standpoint.

Journal Entry

Keep the mind's eye
occupied on the
many real-life
issues or it
quickly attempts to
turn the mundane
into meaningful
comment.

22

THE EMOTIONAL MANAGEMENT SYSTEM
BECOMES SECOND NATURE

The more dedicated you are and the more frequently you use the Emotional Management System, the more profoundly it will merge with your consciousness.

The most rewarding experience for me occurs when people who have learned and applied the Emotional Management System say that their lives have truly changed as a result. These people know that they are using the system but they can't remember actually going through the specific steps one by one anymore. They have reached a level of integration and natural realignment operating on a subconscious level.

That is the fun part for me. The harder part is helping people understand that while the Emotional Management System will introduce seamless integration into their lives, it won't happen right away. It's one of the most important messages to get across, because without your fully appreciating the importance of trying it and trying it and trying it, the Emotional Management System will do very little for you.

THE EMOTIONAL MANAGEMENT SYSTEM IS NOT
A MICROWAVE OVEN

The Emotional Management System isn't meant to generate instant results. To get this point across, I tell people the following story:

Mr. Warrick, an older man who had completed his Witz Training program about a month before, asked me how to apply the Emotional Management System to the marriage break-up he was going through.

We reviewed the Emotional Management System together, studying each step. "Oh, I've done all that" he told me emphatically. "I did it this morning. Nothing's changed." Warrick was looking for—and expected—instant resolution to a highly complex and long-term problem. As I was listening to him, I remembered an incident at Mr. Grant's store in South Africa that always makes me smile, and I suddenly realized that it applied nicely to Warrick's plight. The story helped him get the most out of the Emotional Management System:

Mr. Ron Arnette (Mr. A, we used to call him) walked through the door of the electronics shop one day. He was an impeccably dressed lawyer who worked in an office located a few doors away from us. Recently divorced, he was now living alone. Apparently for the first time, he was doing some of his own cooking and cleaning. Anyway, he marched into the shop with an electric kettle under his arm that he had bought from us the day before, a very stern look on his face.

Mr. Grant: Can I help you?
Mr. A: Yes, indeed. Your kettle doesn't work.
Mr. Grant: What do you mean, it doesn't work?
Mr. A: It doesn't work. I'm trying to make tea with it, but it doesn't work. It just doesn't work.
Mr. Grant: Let me test it and make sure. If there's something wrong with it, I'll give you a new one.

Mr. Grant took the kettle to the back room and tested it. Sure enough, it worked fine. Confidently, he reassured Mr. A and sent him on his way. The next day Mr. A. was back again.

Mr. Grant: Hi, Mr. A. Is the kettle working okay?
Mr. A: Ah, no. Not at all. I don't know what's wrong with it, but I'm telling you, Bob, it just doesn't work.
Mr. Grant: Hold on, I'll check it again.

This time, Mr. Grant came back after a few minutes with the kettle in hand, steam pouring from the spout. Then he poured water into a mug to show that the appliance was working fine. Mr. Grant didn't leave it there, though. He asked Mr. A a few questions.

Mr. Grant: Do you fill the kettle up to the line with water?
Mr. A: I do indeed.
Mr. Grant: Do you make sure that the kettle is plugged in?
Mr. A: Of course I do.
Mr. Grant: Do you switch the kettle on?
Mr. A: Absolutely!
Mr. Grant: I know. Maybe the socket you're using is dead.
Mr. A: Nope, it isn't. I use the outlet for my toaster and that works all the time.

Mr. Grant was stumped. He asked Mr. A to explain how he used the kettle. Mr. A went through all the steps, up to and including pouring in the cold water, which he filled to the brim, and turning on the kettle.

Mr. Grant: So then what do you do?
Mr. A: Well, I switch it on, then I wait. Nothing happens, it just gets warm. One time I waited nearly two minutes, and still the water never got more than mildly hot. I can't drink tea that way. So, after that, I unplug the kettle because it doesn't work.
Mr. Grant: Oh. Well, actually, Mr. A, a kettle is not like a toaster.

Mr. Grant realized that Mr. A had likely never boiled water before. In his remarkably restrained and polite way Mr. Grant then explained how to boil water, telling Mr. A that it can take a little time to bring the water to a boil, especially when you fill the kettle with cold water right to the top.

When I was finished telling him the story, Mr. Warrick nodded in understanding. We talked for a while about the Emotional Management System and how, like using a kettle to boil water, the resolution to an issue requires the patience to allow correct procedures to effect transformation. We discussed how some, if not all, of the steps will have to be repeated again and again when first beginning the process. With each repetition, however, you begin to find how natural it is to use your existing skills in this focused way until you have met your objective. But most of all, the Emotional Management System takes time.

Journal Entry

Ignorance is most often accompanied
by outrage . . .
giving the mistaken impression
of intelligent righteousness.

23

MAINTAINING CAVEBRAIN-COMPUTERBRAIN ALIGNMENT

Many situations become emotionally charged and lead to a negative outcome. Fear encourages either non-action or reckless and rushed action as you try getting yourself out of the situation as quickly as possible. Such was the case with Christopher, an Emotional Management System student.

Chris has a compulsion for always doing the right thing. He was punctual for all his classes at the training centre, and he was never unprepared. He is also very sensitive, prone to reacting before thinking, which was one of the reasons he enrolled in the program.

Chris's perceptions are influenced by the cavebrain reactions generated by his internal predisposition. The story he told everyone during the session, therefore, was very instructive.

Chris's story:

> Most people carry unnecessary baggage of some kind. In my case it's what I have come to call an illogical fear of criticism.
>
> Like most people, I do not enjoy criticism. No, change that: I detest criticism. Let me take you back to a day last fall. I am an administrative manager and report to Noah, a vice-president of the company I work for.
>
> On this particular morning I was late arriving at my office. An accident on the highway had caused a traffic jam for more than half an hour. It was approximately 10:45 when I walked in. With a knowing look, my assistant handed me two messages from the company president. The first read: "10:00 a.m. Please call." The second read: "10:30 a.m. Please call. Urgent."

The two messages had arrived within half an hour of each other and I interpreted an unspoken but very evident tone questioning my punctuality. I felt attacked. I became angry. My spirits sank and my stomach tightened. It sounds silly, but I actually began to feel quite sick.

I thought to myself, "Great, just great. Three weeks in a row I am here by 8:00 a.m. He doesn't send me messages then, does he! Today he calls. What a great way to start the day. Well, I might as well get this over with."

This kind of frustrating interpersonal situation happens to us frequently. Chris is emotional. He allows his feelings to run wild. Not unlike most people who react this way, he becomes a victim and feels that he is not appreciated. He seeks approval and praise which, according to him, he never receives. If, however, there is a criticism about him or his work, he then believes that plenty is being said about him, none of it positive or supportive.

As Chris reads the messages, he becomes increasingly frustrated. This frustration turns to anger as he considers his past performance. After all, every day he arrives early and his boss never called first thing in the morning then. Today he is late through no fault of his own and his boss has called him two times first thing in the morning. Somehow the whole thing doesn't seem fair. Chris's emotions are dictating his perception and subsequent actions. Chris's approach is likely to generate a negative outcome.

How should Chris react? Consider this: his reaction is based primarily on an assumption. He has not heard what his boss has to say. He has simply read two messages that he interpreted to say: "Call me as soon as you get in. It's 9:45, where are you?"

Chris continues:

If I persisted in operating from my cavebrain mode, the situation probably would have gone as follows:

(I phone Noah)

Noah (a little abrupt): Noah speaking.
Me: Good morning, Noah, Chris here. I believe you are looking for me.
Noah: Yes, I was. Where were you this morning?
Me: There was an accident on the way in. It held me up. Why?

Me (thinking): Do I have to report to this guy every second of the day?
Me: I'm in most mornings before eight, I don't see any messages then!
Noah: You sound a bit uptight this morning, Chris. Is there something wrong?
Me (thinking): You're damn right, you son of a bitch.

Chris makes his sense of victimization apparent. Chris is in pure cavebrain survival mode, trying to protect his self-esteem which he believes is being attacked. He has used no strategies to integrate his computerbrain with his cavebrain.

Noah, for his part, must be wondering why Chris is behaving so antagonistically, and he is probably going to get pretty reactive himself.

In his cavebrain anger, Chris becomes reckless. His taunting has done little to help him in this situation. His approach and manner is based on perception rather than fact. Through his reckless actions, he risks creating a reality that will comply with his preconceptions and lead to a negative outcome.

Chris has learned to deal with most situations in this inappropriate manner. Looking so desperately for an opportunity to rid himself of his frustration, he risks creating even more problems for himself. Chris is in a no-win situation.

At this point, he feels that he has in no way contributed to the problems unfolding. Unless he uses another approach, he will conclude that he has been manipulated by a person or by circumstances beyond his control. He will only succeed in jeopardizing his position. Once this happens, he reinforces his belief that he is, ultimately, the victim.

We have all been in a similar position to Chris's, when the prospect of going to find out the facts can be as stressful in the short term as discovering that your perception was actually correct. We often terrorize ourselves with speculations that play themselves out in our minds and are usually far worse than the potential confrontation could ever be. Some people even end up putting themselves through extended emotional turmoil by avoiding the issue.

Chris had a long history of quitting. He was prompted to come to learn the Emotional Management System when he recognized a recurring pattern that maintained a destructive status quo.

Chris needs to minimize his desire to react. He must STOP. At this stage he can only speculate, but he must resist the temptation to do so. Once he calls his boss, he will be able to begin to deal with the situation.

For all Chris knows, his boss may not even mention Chris's lateness. Noah may have a much more pressing problem to discuss with him.

In a situation like Chris's, and considering his sensitivity, there is an enormous temptation to speculate. But if you give in to this temptation, you risk reacting to what you perceive is going to happen. Chris did not give in.

Chris goes on:

> What follows is what really ended up happening as I applied the Emotional Management System.
>
> The two messages had arrived within half an hour of each other, and I interpreted an unspoken but very evident tone questioning my punctuality.

Me (thinking): Hang on a second, Chris, STOP a minute. But I'm angry. No "but." STOP, STOP, I MUST STOP! Settle down for a moment. Relax. If I'm going to do battle, I had at least better get ready. Okay, how do I get ready? Well, I've already taken the first step of the Emotional Management System: I've STOPPED. Phew, that's a first! Okay, so far, so good. What next?

This is the internalization of the Emotional Management System. Chris has managed to STOP long enough to permit a logical approach. Don't underestimate just how difficult it is to actually STOP. It requires commitment and discipline. By STOPPING, Chris is able to pause long enough to recognize that he wants to let his computerbrain provide input so that he can reach his PI.

Once Chris STOPS, he can control himself and avoid reacting in a spontaneous way that may result in an unfavourable outcome. From a STOPPED position he can instigate a computerbrain approach to the situation.

Chris has STOPPED. He is now ready for the second step. He is ready to LISTEN.

Me (thinking): Okay, what is Noah saying? He said, "Please call. Urgent." Yes, but what did he really mean?

Wait, wait, I must STOP again. I must answer the question. What is the question? What is Noah saying? He said, "Please call. Urgent."

What Chris has effectively managed to do so far is concentrate on listening to what has been said—in this case, he is actually listening to what has been written. He has also prevented his cavebrain from immediately leaping to its self-protective opinions and overtaking the situation.

Me (thinking): "Please call. Urgent." Nothing else. Well, that's not too bad. No blood's been shed yet. Okay, so what's the next step? I must maintain my Position of Independence. Step 3: Research. Research what? There's no one to check with on something like this. Or is there?

Most of us get very confused when it comes to Step 3. Chris's initial reaction is that there is no one to check with. He is not sure how to research. When you research, you are gathering bits of information. The more questions you ask, the better.

Me (thinking): How do I research this? I want to treat this situation in a professional manner. The more questions I ask, the more facts I will unveil. Who can I ask? Answer: in this case, only myself.

Okay, self, what are the facts as I see them? Is there any damage of any kind so far? None that I am aware of.

Have I experienced any previous problems in this area of present concern? No!

Have I broken any rules? None to my knowledge.

Has the company suffered in any way due to me being late today? I might need to check this further when I speak to Noah.

Well, I can't do any more research other than to phone and speak to Noah. The only other person who can reveal more facts is Noah. That's the next step.

Now is the time for me to move to Step 4: Update my own opinion. In my opinion, I have done nothing wrong. Hmm. But why am I panicking, then? Stop, Chris, don't lose it now. Okay, where was I? I was thinking that in my opinion I have done nothing wrong. Moreover, based on my research so far, it is possible that my concerns have no foundation. Right, next step. Step 5: Weigh the pros and cons. Then, Step 6: Define my objective.

Weighing the pros and cons is a re-evaluation process of the information generated by the first four steps of the Emotional Management System. Prior to defining what you want to achieve and what you want to do, you examine and balance all the facts, or lack thereof; you determine whether your objective is positively or negatively charged; and you give yourself the opportunity to approach the situation logically and decide whether or not more work is required in any of the previous steps. You are now operating from an integrated cavebrain-computerbrain position to define your objective.

Let's continue Chris's story:

> The pro of the situation is that so far I really recognize that I am overreacting. There is no evidence so far that anything is actually wrong. I am not living in real time. I am allowing past perceptions to dictate my feelings and reactions today.
>
> Now, what about the cons? I honestly can't think of any other than that if I make my feelings apparent, I can almost guarantee that I will create some major trouble for myself with Noah.
>
> Now, what is my objective? My objective is to return Noah's calls and find out what's on his mind. Gosh, that sounds almost too simple.

Chris is, in fact, 100 percent right. It does seem almost too simple. The truth is, in most cases it *is* that simple. It is through your cavebrain's self-protective survival-based reaction that you overcomplicate most situations. Chris now moves to Step 7: GO.

(Chris calls Noah.)

Noah: Hello.
Me: Good morning, Noah. How are you this morning?
Noah: I'm okay, Chris. How are you?
Me: Great, thanks. I got your messages. . . .
Noah: Yes, where were you this morning, Chris?
Me: (thinking) STOP. Don't get hooked! It's only a question.
Me: There was an accident on the way in. It held me up.

Chris's voice is relaxed. His tone is not sarcastic. From his PI he is able to deal rationally with the situation. He can deal rationally with it because he has options that he gained by integrating his computerbrain's input with his cavebrain's reaction in order to obtain the most accurate perspective on all facets of his situation. He is able to listen to what Noah is asking without interjecting his own opinion. He is not corrupting his listening abilities with preconceptions.

Chris: You said in your messages that it was urgent. What can I do to help, Noah?
Noah: Yes, sorry to bother you first thing. I'm desperate for this week's production numbers . . .

Because you were not personally involved in Chris's situation—and unless you have had a similar experience—it may be difficult for you to fully appreciate the anxiety that entrapped Chris when he first read the messages his assistant handed to him. Furthermore, after reviewing the interaction between Chris and his boss, you may be inclined to underestimate its complexity and find yourself observing only the simplicity involved in ultimately dealing with the interaction.

To get a better idea of the realities of this kind of situation, think back to a situation that bothered you enormously. Or better yet, consider a difficult situation that you are faced with now. With this in mind, you will be able to recognize and appreciate how, when your emotions swing into gear, a simple situation can quickly become complicated. When this happens, you recognize how your imagination creates various scenarios, resulting in your contemplating all kinds of gut-wrenching and unproductive thoughts that, in turn, produces the kind of emotional intelligence pattern that leads to trouble.

Consider how quickly you begin to complicate the situation, not unlike Chris who, without any forethought, initially permitted his cave-brain perceptions to colour and generate the facts of the situation. With your PI in place you can avoid unnecessary complications, and highly charged emotional situations actually become simple to deal with. In some instances, you are able to handle a situation in minutes instead of months.

This reminds me of an Emotional Management System student who became increasingly disenchanted with her job and her boss. Her belief that her boss was a monster grew daily. After discussing her predicament with me, she was quick to offer, as one alternative to her problem, that she quit her job. This was an alternative that she had contemplated many times over the past eighteen months.

Her predicament so intimidated her that her first reaction was to remain transfixed in a cycle of indecision and non-action. Through the Emotional Management System, she steadily worked through her situation, evaluating each facet point by point. Only after she reached a Position of Independence was she able to begin to interact with her boss.

The entire interaction between her and me took a total of four minutes. Subsequently when I spoke to her, the first thing she said was how simple the whole thing was. She ended by saying, "What was all the fuss about?"

Your Position of Independence is the method that proportionately simplifies your situation. I say proportionately because all situations, of course, are not equal in intensity or complexity.

Chris successfully used the Emotional Management System to reach his PI. Without the Emotional Management System, the entire interaction with his boss could have gone completely awry. But it didn't. Chris might have agonized unnecessarily for hours. But he didn't. He integrated his computerbrain and cavebrain with the Emotional Management System so that he could reach his Position of Independence. From that position, he was able to respond to his boss naturally and intelligently, and prevent himself from behaving in a self-defeating manner.

NATURAL PATIENCE, INSTINCTIVE FOCUS

Dr. Rajan is an eye surgeon. Before he learned the Emotional Management System, he had a hair-trigger temper. At the slightest provocation or even hint of provocation, he would blow up and make life miserable for everyone around him, and most of all, for himself. He recounted the following interaction at his eye clinic:

Mr. Lanzarotta: Dr. Rajan, I'm having trouble reading. I think I need glasses.
Dr. Rajan: Do you have any trouble seeing objects in the distance?
Mr. Lanzarotta: No.
Dr. Rajan: Do you do any special type of work?
Mr. Lanzarotta: No.
Dr. Rajan: Any double vision?
Mr. Lanzarotta: Hey, Doctor, I just want my eyes tested. I really don't have the time or inclination for all these questions. I know what I need. I just need glasses to read, that's all. For crying out loud, can we just get on with this thing?

Dr. Rajan could easily have allowed his emotions to be triggered by the patient's belligerent attitude. He instantly became aware of the need to consciously STOP and apply the Emotional Management System to the situation. He does not automatically accept the obvious even though he deals with the "obvious" on a daily basis. In this particular case it is just as well that he doesn't allow the patient's tunnel vision to dictate his approach.

Dr. Rajan: Mr. Lanzarotta, I'm sorry that you are getting upset, but I need to ask you a lot of questions about your lifestyle and your general health, because your eyes may reflect the state of your health. I don't want to overlook any serious problem. If you can hold on for just a couple of minutes, could you assist me by answering a few more questions? Then I promise, I will test you immediately for the glasses you need.
Mr. Lanzarotta: Well, all right, if you think it's important. I apologize. I didn't mean to be rude. I guess I've been very edgy these days.
Dr. Rajan: That's okay. Tell me, have you been getting any headaches lately?
Mr. Lanzarotta: Yes, quite often.
Dr. Rajan: Even at night?
Mr. Lanzarotta: Yes.
Dr. Rajan: Do you find that they wake you up at night?
Mr. Lanzarotta: Sometimes.
Dr. Rajan: Do you ever vomit when you have these headaches?
Mr. Lanzarotta: A couple of times, I suppose. But I thought it had something to do with my diet.
Dr. Rajan: Any double vision?
Mr. Lanzarotta: Yes, when I get these headaches. I'm really quite fine the rest of the time, so I haven't paid much attention to them.
Dr. Rajan: I'm just going to put these drops in your eyes. They take about twenty minutes to work. Then we'll chat more about the headaches and see about the glasses.

How often do you accept the "obvious" conclusions that others place before you, especially when you have grown accustomed to this practice? When you don't STOP and you accept a situation and your position without question, you can cause irreparable harm.

As it turned out, Dr. Rajan's examination showed that Mr. Lanzarotta was suffering from bilateral swelling of the optic nerves, indicating a possible brain tumour. X-rays later confirmed this. Surgery was required to save Mr. Lanzarotta's life. He was admitted to the hospital immediately and an operation was carried out successfully.

Not all STOP concepts and PI's have this dramatic a result. The patient's condition no doubt contributed to his short-tempered cavebrain behaviour. If Dr. Rajan had let his emotions towards the patient alter his usual examination procedure and had he permitted the patient to manipulate him into a quick eye examination, the results could have had extremely unfortunate consequences for the patient.

However, Dr. Rajan had been using the Emotional Management System for more than two years and had assimilated the technique to the point where he did not have to remind himself of the specific steps. Instead of becoming reactive and weathering the rudeness of his patient by giving him a regular eye exam, he was able to easily handle the interaction and allow his experience and intuition to prompt him to examine the patient further.

This is an important corollary benefit that the Emotional Management System produces: expanded insight. People who successfully use the Emotional Management System constantly report the surprising results that they achieve, beyond their initial reason for learning the system. These are the kinds of results you can expect in your life as well.

EPILOGUE

Transformation is absolutely possible. I have seen the Emotional Management System work for countless people. There are so many stories, so many happy endings, so many people who have learned the system and followed it, to discover the importance of self-reliance and self-respect.

The achievements of individuals give me a deep sense of satisfaction and great joy. In fact, I do not think I could ask for a more personally satisfying profession. I am grateful to have been able to develop an understanding of how emotions and perceptions affect everything we do. This understanding has enabled me to develop the Emotional Management System.

The system does not require you to do anything you are incapable of doing, or that you would be uncomfortable doing. It teaches you to manage your emotions. And when you learn how to manage your emotions, you develop the capacity to engage your computerbrain in a way that produces genuinely fulfilling solutions in your life.

You now have the tools to make sound and wise interpersonal decisions. Most of all, you are being responsible to yourself, freeing yourself from the self-sabotaging dictates of your cavebrain and letting yourself integrate rational thought in your decisions and actions. The result is your Position of Independence: a balanced approach to life that enables you to make decisions and take the action necessary to fulfil your ultimate personal goals. This is your freedom.

My wish and expectation is that you learn to follow this simple system and make your life more harmonious and successful than you dared dream possible.

APPENDIX

THE EMOTIONAL MANAGEMENT SYSTEM IN ACTION

PERSONAL ACCOUNTS

Gerald Burger

You never know what is in store for you. It is not until you are on the brink of losing everything that you appreciate what you have.

Things can change in an instant. At one moment you find yourself happily married, in a job, living in suburbia, and then, suddenly, a single idea leads to changes that can turn your life around.

My then-wife wanted to return to her native New Zealand. She had never really accepted living in North America. She often reminisced about how much better, safer, and cleaner New Zealand was. I always thought of it as the remotest part of the world. But as is often the case, persistence and perhaps fear of loss can be heady persuaders. She relentlessly pursued the idea of our emigrating to New Zealand. Although I was not initially enthusiastic about the prospect, I finally agreed. We sold our house, withdrew our savings, and cashed in our insurance policies. With a tidy but modest sum of money, we set off to start a new life.

I didn't realize it at the time, but I was about to say goodbye to everything that was familiar to me. One ignorantly believes that if you go from one English-speaking country to another, the transition can't be all that difficult. Ignorance is bliss only until reality smashes its full force into your consciousness. The first few weeks in my newly adopted country were enchanting. I was fortunate enough to find a timber merchant eager to sell his business. Although I knew nothing about being a timber merchant, I had always dreamed of being my own boss, and this opportunity seemed ideal. The owner of the business, a riley old weatherbeaten New Zealander, was retiring. He built up my expectations with his proud tales and memories. As I listened to him I convinced myself that I could handle the challenges and steadily build up the business. After examining the books, I believed this was not only possible but that I could make one hell of a go of it. My wife and I bought the business by taking out a sizeable chunk of our savings and mortgaging the assets to the bank. And that is how I became the proud owner of my very own timber business.

It didn't take very long for reality to set in. Perhaps it was the combination of finding myself in a strange culture, and the owner of a new business, together with a yearning for the familiar that made things more difficult than they should have been. The business did not go as I had expected or planned. Things started to go wrong very quickly and within six months I found myself in hospital suffering from severe depression. I was also told that I was a candidate for a heart attack.

It was while lying in hospital at the lowest ebb I have ever been in my life that I remembered the training I received at Witz. I can honestly say that the act of stopping and initiating the simple yet powerfully logical steps I learned at those training sessions probably saved my life.

I was soon discharged from the hospital. We lost the business and, as is often the case, my wife and I turned on each other. I would like to believe that I could have found a way to fix it all, but the odds were stacked against me. Thank goodness the one thing I could rely on was my inner self. I returned to my native land alone, with the daunting prospect of starting all over again with nothing.

My Witz training allowed me to stop the panic and know that I had to—and could—rely on myself. The Emotional Management System helped me to navigate one tiny step at a time. There are no quick fixes. There are no easy answers. This systematic approach taught me how to harness my resources.

Time is a great healer and I'm now remaking my life. I will never know what might have been had I not had the Emotional Management System to guide me. Perhaps all I can say is that thank god I did.

Rose Maslen

My first marriage was a disaster. My next ex-husband was pure charm. He charmed me right into marrying him and working for him in his company. And he was so charming that he thought I wouldn't notice that he was still seeing his former wife.

To make himself look good, he began a campaign to make me look bad, telling everyone (including me) that I was insanely jealous, with no cause to be. He even convinced me I needed psychiatric help. I became so depressed, I started to take anti-depressants. I even threatened suicide, just to try to get something to change.

Through all this turmoil, I continued to be aware of my husband's infidelity. My accusations only enraged him further, making matters worse for me. After one frightening altercation with my husband, when I was sure he was about to seriously hurt me, I packed my bags and left. I had reached the end of my rope.

We separated immediately, and I was suddenly alone and wondering what I was going to do with my life. That was six years ago. Fortunately, I learned about the Emotional Management System, signed up for the training sessions, and became a new person.

The course gave me insights into many aspects of myself. It helped me see that as a child, I always tried to please my parents, ingratiating myself to make sure they loved me. I was obedient and self-effacing, unwilling to offer an opinion for fear it would antagonize someone.

The Emotional Management System has helped me immensely. Now, many years after learning the program, I see remarkable growth in myself. My self-esteem is fully restored, perhaps even in better shape than it has ever been. I realized that just because my second ex-husband chose to be unfaithful, it didn't mean I wasn't a worthwhile person, or that I wasn't desirable or attractive. In fact, I've never had a better or more meaningful social life. And people who know me say that my entire demeanour is different. I'm not the withdrawn person so afraid to speak her mind.

The program was so inspiring that after I learned the Emotional Management System, I enrolled in law school and became a trial lawyer. As a lawyer I use both discretion and assertiveness to get my points across. This new assertiveness has emerged as a result of my learning the system.

I've been using the Emotional Management System in my practice for years. Its precepts have become second nature.

A lot of people who were in law school with me were petrified of going into court and arguing their cases. They didn't have the training that the Emotional Management System gives you to maintain control and focus. I do have it. That's my competitive advantage. I know what my clients' objectives are, I know what their position is, and I know what they're entitled to and what they're not entitled to. I'm able to go in there and present their case in the best possible light. So, even though I'm not nearly as experienced as most of the lawyers I face, I feel I still have that advantage.

I remember my first case. The lawyer I was up against was a legend. I started to feel intimidated, but then I STOPPED, examined the situation, and realized that I was totally prepared for the case, and I knew exactly how I was going to present it. In very short order, I regained my confidence. I won my first case.

Sandy O'Reilly

The Emotional Management System changed my life. It helped me realize my professional goals and personal dreams. It is, in a word, transformative.

The company I work for, Nissan Canada, sent me and a number of my colleagues to Witz Training to learn how to become better managers. The course turned out to be so much more. For me it was about renewing myself. In fact, the program inspired me to do something I had always wanted to do but had never allowed myself to consider: run a marathon.

As a result of one of the exercises, I learned that we limit ourselves in achieving our goals. I learned the extent to which I limit myself. I decided to make my dream come true by expanding the limits I had set for myself, those boundaries that kept me a prisoner of my preconceptions. I decided I *would* run a marathon. On went the sneakers and sweat suit, and off I went on a nightly run. I also joined a fitness group that was focused on running and preparing for marathons.

I started training with a modest goal: if I could run 10 kilometres by the end of the summer I would be really pleased. By mid-July I had completed a 20-kilometre run, and decided to set a new objective—the full marathon, 26 miles, 385 yards. Witz Training took me through the seven steps of the Emotional Management System to the point in my personal development where I *knew* I could run a marathon. I *knew* I could realize my dream.

The day of the annual Canadian International Marathon was warm and sunny and calm. My objective was to finish. That's what the Emotional Management System does for you. It lets you see what you want to accomplish and then helps you use the tools you naturally possess to realize your objectives.

I took my last stride, crossed the line, and couldn't wipe the smile off my face for a very long time. I had run a marathon. I felt a tremendous sense of accomplishment.

I've been on a high ever since. I now look at my professional dreams the same way as I looked at my personal dreams: as real possibilities and opportunities. Take performance reviews for example. This kind of interaction is frequently stressful for both parties. As the person conducting the evaluation, you need to stay focused on your objective, while remaining sensitive to the sometimes highly charged emotions of the person being evaluated. This is where you apply the Emotional Management System in a dynamic way so that each party in the interaction comes away undiminished.

Learning the Emotional Management System is a profoundly powerful experience. During the intensive program, you suddenly realize things about yourself that you never considered before. Frequently these insights into yourself are not pleasant or flattering, but they are transformative. And that's what the system does: it lets you be who you really are, strong and powerful.

Having learned to apply the Emotional Management System, I find myself more attuned to my colleagues. I have learned to stop and listen; I have learned to communicate more effectively. I am a better manager because I am now able to help people consider their potential. I can help people view themselves in a new way. The Emotional Management System has helped me become comfortable with who I am. My personal growth started with running the marathon. I realized, however, that running the marathon really wasn't about running; it was about believing in myself. The Emotional Management System opened my eyes to the fact that all of it—my professional goals, my personal dreams—was really about believing in myself.

INDEX

 WITZ TRAINING

Witz Training Programs—
Improving Lives for More Than 25 Years

Paul Witz and his seasoned team of facilitators have provided more than 10,000 individuals with powerful one-on-one interpersonal training. Witz Training offers courses based on the company's simple, powerful, and complete learning system. Over its 25 years of research—and more than 20 years of applied teaching—Witz Training has developed programs to help individuals and businesses succeed.

Program 1. The Essentials—
a 12-week training in self-esteem, communication,
and assertiveness

In-depth training in the three essential building blocks of interpersonal success: self-esteem, communication, and assertiveness. Three action formulas are the foundation of this training: 1. Establishing Your Position of Independence; 2. Controlling Communication; and 3. Natural Assertiveness. Also available as a 7-cassette audio training series and as a 10-cassette video training series.

Program 2. BizCom—
the communication foundation of successful business

This course gives you the superior interpersonal skills necessary to inspire and motivate colleagues and employees, to problem-solve, and to communicate dynamically with those both inside and outside your organization. BizCom is the strategic solution that can make an organization more competitive and its personnel more effective.

Program 3. PresCom—complete presentation skills training

A presentation is a performance during which the audience judges performer, dialogue, mood, intent, and subject. For whatever kind of presentation you're called upon to make, and to whatever size group, PresCom provides the comprehensive knowledge you need to master this core business skill.

http://www.witztraining.com